CELTIC HIGH CROSSES
OF WALES

Celtic High Crosses of Wales

John Sharkey

GWASG Carreg Gwalch

ISBN: 0-86381-489-1

Cover design: Smala, Caernarfon

First published in 1998 by Gwasg Carreg Gwalch,
12 Iard yr Orsaf, Llanrwst, Wales LL26 0EH
☎ (01492) 642031
Printed and published in Wales.

Contents

Illustrations of the crosses are included throughout the book.

Acknowledgements

To Claire, AnaRose, Sam and Biddy for their cheerful forbearance during the writing.

To Maura Hazelden for her support and help with all the illustrations that are such an essential part of the book. And for the inclusion of her drawings, photographs and maps.

To Micky Baines for the use of his photographs of the Llanbadarn Fawr and Carew crosses.

To Elizabeth Cox for her map of the medieval pilgrim routes.

To O.S. Westwood for whose reproductions from *Lapidarium Walliae* are still probably the clearest in terms of design and an indication of what many crosses may have looked like in the early 19th century.

To Gareth Evans, librarian and staff of Cardigan Public Library.

To Comisiwn Brenhinol Henebion Cymru for their kind permission to reproduce the illustration of Burry Holms from the Glamorgan Inventory.

To the University of Wales Press for their kind permission to reprint the Gododdin stanza from A Guide to Welsh Literature, Vol. 1, Edited by A.O.H. Jarman and Gwilym Rees Hughes.

To the Leicester University Press (a Cassell imprint), London, all rights reserved, for their kind permission to reprint the *englyn* to Padarn's staff from Wales in the Early Middle Ages by Wendy Davies.

Part 1

Religious and Cultural Background

Summary

The themes engaged upon in this overview of three areas of Wales, the south, the west and the north, can be briefly stated. First and the most important, deals with the perception of the Christian cross as it emerged in western Britain during the immediate post-Roman period. The cross in its main iconic forms found on stone, was the *chi-rho* monogram as on the Penmachno stone in Gwynedd, the Latin cross devoid of the monogram elements which from the seventh-century on had as many different forms and variations as have been found on the mass of Class 2 cross-slabs, and finally the Greek wheeled-cross, latterly known as the Celtic ring-cross. The most pertinent example is on the large boulder from Castell Dwyran in Carmarthenshire. Its MEMORIA VOTEPORIGIS PROTICTORIS inscription with the name also in Ogam below the cross carving, dated it to the middle of the sixth-century. The Irish and Latin forms with the Roman epithet indicate a local cultural integration at this period. However the large pillar stone as a memorial to the dead harks back to the Bronze Age and shows the continuance of ancient burial traditions.

There is a distinct gap in time and scale before the small slab carvings of simple ring and Latin crosses became generally used as grave-markers. In Ireland these often had names inscribed in insular half-uncial and minuscule lettering whereas the Group 2 slabs in Wales, dated from the seventh to the ninth-centuries, have crosses but are otherwise uninscribed.

Both the ringed-cross and the Latin cross, sometimes with the alpha and omega added, may have initially evolved from the *chi-rho* monogram. However the paucity of material evidence and the lack of it in other media such as wood or metal, as well as the conflicting views of

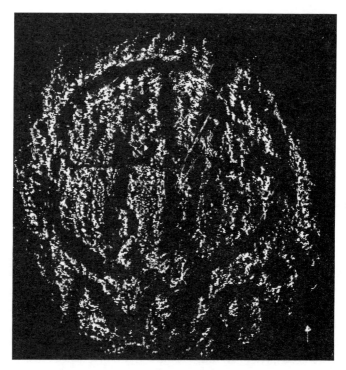

Rubbing (half-size) of ringed-cross on Castell Dwyran stone,
now in Carmarthen Museum. (Photograph by M.H.)

art historians, make any typological progression relating either in time or to place, untenable. Even though the earliest examples of the above types found on ceramics in post-Roman Britain that have been dated from the early fifth-century to the period of the Vortipor stone a century or so later, the cross-forms have been found so widely and clearly from different cultural groups that to link such Christian symbols as a whole is as misleading as the suggestion that they demonstrate a chronology of Christianity here.

The fact is that even prior to trading activity in and around the western maritime province, Christianity was marginal to the wider European church. The three British bishops sent to the Council of Rimini in 359 had to rely on official handouts indicating the poverty of the church even then. A sharp contrast to the ecclesiastical wealth elsewhere in the empire which grew from endowments, offerings – often called first fruits – and revenue from rents. The extensive range of Roman Christian art in church architecture, on portable objects and on other media, from the middle of the fourth-century onwards is noticeably absent in Britain.

Irish heritage is more fortunate in this respect but Wales is lacking in church remains earlier than the Norman era. This is one reason why the early stone crosses and later decorated high cross constitute the single most important body of evidence of Christian activity here. Yet it still remains something of an anomaly in Dark Age historical and religious studies.

A stumbling block may be the chronology and classification by Nash-Williams which has been largely accepted almost without question since it was published in 1950. Something of a sacred cow! One recent exception is a critical examination by Ken Dark. He concluded that art history, epigraphy and dubious historical associations do not enable a detailed chronology for the early monuments to be accepted without question and that the use of such monuments as a key to conventional dating in pre-Norman Wales is of doubtful value.

It would be equally rash to ascribe an evolutionary link between these early stone crosses with the shaped cross or cross carved in relief to any 'final liberation' of the up-standing high cross. The Irish ringed high cross which may or may not have been influenced by a lineage of artisans in Northumbria and the Inner Hebrides, seems to have materialized fully formed in the late eight-century. The carving of the free-standing crosses in Wales has been dated from the late ninth to eleventh centuries, by which time the particular styles of abstract carving that we usually call Celtic would have been the common repertoire of masons and certainly familiar to their commissioners.

The second theme is the manner in which our early Christianity as it manifested in western Britain had been recorded by medieval historians. They would have been familiar both with the old religious landscape and the newer cultural milieu. It is also possible that the traditional forms of the saintly hagiography – a sort of fabulous biographical gloss on the life of founder saints – may have been read or recited in Welsh in monastic and church settings long before they were written down in manuscript Latin. Clearly attempting to preserve what they considered important from the past in a form that was consistent with church rather than the literary history, then becoming increasingly popular with a secular readership.

However this late medieval understanding and setting of the life and times of the Celtic saints with its inference on the monastic role-model, has been seriously questioned by modern scholars. In many ways this has become an exercise in pedantry for it does not seem to add much to the overall knowledge of the period whether one opts for the so-called Celtic Church as opposed to the academically correct term, the Early Christian church in Wales.

A recent study of Early Christian art, referring to how the 'new' images of Christ affected the way people 'thought' and that once they 'imagined' Christ he 'became' what they pictured him to be, points out the three ways by which historians have managed to ignore the revolutionary changes of the fourth and fifth-centuries. In relation to the power of such images the first method was to deny their validity by subsuming them into a neutral 'art' category. Another way was to concentrate on the form rather than the content of the image. The third shift comes about when the new imagery is finally confronted but in using a term like 'iconography', "its special energy and power in the competition with pagan imagery is not raised". (Mathews, 1993)

This seems to me to be close to how modern scholars portray the spread of Christianity in western Britain. And especially in relation to the 'new' image or symbol of the cross. It began as an exotic import from the east but by the seventh-century it had infiltrated the natural pagan landscape to such a degree that the cross carved on a piece of stone symbolized not only the death of Christ but his resurrection and his teachings. As a marker on or by a banked enclosure, it also proclaimed his church here and now! On this spot, on this earth! It was an extraordinary change brought about in an entirely rural unliterate Celtic environment. Rather than engaging with such a primal and primary perception, the power of the cross is quietly ignored in a kind of intellectual lay-by from which its abstract image can be brought out to prove a point or when an illustration is needed.

The process can be seen clearly in the 'Romanization' of the spread of Christianity in that part of Britain we now call modern Wales. There is no archaeological or other material evidence to support the assertion that the forts or small towns were even nominally Christian and that after the legions departed the roads were the avenues by which the new faith spread. In fact even in the extreme south-eastern region where Christianity is said to have radiated out from in the immediate post-Roman period, the church dedications to a saint like *Dubricious*, or Dyfrig, are all retrospectively based on late medieval material. So on the one hand, saintly hagiography is considered unhistorical but it can be used with 'consideration' when site dedications appear approximately close (mapwise) to a Roman road. That such tracks were used by local people is not in question rather it is the unproven suggestion of the footsteps of the saints that is used to bolster the current theory and where use of the word 'Roman' in discussion has almost become a court of final appeal.

The need to rationalize and ultimately deny the Celticism that antiquarians and an earlier generation of historians like Chatwick, Dillon, Jackson and others used as the basis of native Christian art and religion, is in part a reductive anti-traditional approach to the past. It is a historical trend that is even spreading to Ireland with claims that Roman influence was more intrusive that has been generally supposed. Tacitus' view that his father-in-law could have thrashed the Irish with a few legions has become accepted fact. His colourful account many years after the supposed event of screaming druidesses with their skirts up high holding back the macho Roman army, is pure Hollywood pulp.

More likely to judge from the map of the times, Seutonius Paulinus may even have thought he was invading Ireland, as Anglesey from across the Menai Straits looks like the long side of that triangular shape. Roman writers were masters at manipulating history to their advantage. The metal hoards that were thought to be isolated booty from the British province and dated to different periods of the occupation, are now being used to underwrite a possible Roman settlement at Drumanagh, Co. Dublin, as the spearhead of an aborted invasion. Another scenario puts the use of Ogam back to the third-century. Since the cipher-script is based on Latin, it has been seriously suggested that the language itself must have been in familiar use long before the fifth-century when it was introduced into the south of Ireland, as part of the formal liturgical practice of Christianity.

Ogam is now recognised as the earliest of our ethnic written languages and it was certainly created before it was first used in its monumental form on memorial stones. When this occurred and whether in Ireland or Wales are still open questions. However once the script was formulated, any illiterate mason could chip out a formula on the side of a boulder.

The final theme is, even if one accepts that the Christian faith had a second flowering, so as to speak, in south-east Wales, there seems no good reason to deny the traditional notion of conversion by missionaries who were often born here. Then, after a religious schooling in Gaul was finished off with a pilgrimage to Rome and Jerusalem 'to walk in the footsteps of Christ', they returned to their homelands again dedicated to the task of bringing the light of faith to their pagan fellow Celts. And that this resurgence took place in Wales and Ireland during the fifth and sixth-centuries.

There is certainly a good case to be made that there was a definite evangelical movement into south, west and north Wales by different groups but with a common motivation. In fact Nash-Williams goes so far to suggest that it was part of a deliberate policy of the church in Gaul. By sailing through the western seaways, small monastic enclosures with good water and soil were sited inland along the narrow river valleys for maximum seclusion. The organisation of the later churches that grew from this movement was based on the 'clas' or mother church. A community of men – both priests and lay monks – living together and following a monastic rule under the guidance of an abbot. A 'clas' usually had a hermitage – often on a small island such as Ynys Seiriol opposite Penmon – for the monks to retire to in meditative retreat or in old age. Many of the most important medieval churches originated as 'clasau' and it is in these, such as Llanilltud Fawr (*Llantwit Major*), Nevern, Llanbadarn Fawr and Penmon itself, where some of the outstanding Celtic high crosses were located.

The Three Helens

The traditions of the three saintly Helens encapsulate some popular associations with the advent of Christianity in Wales. Elen Ferch Endaf the British bride of the emperor Maximus returned home after his death, bringing her Christian confessor from Trèves, a monastery in Gaul associated with St Martin of Tours. Helena, the mother of Constantine the Great, has holy well dedications in Wales and especially at St Helens on Merseyside. Sarnau Helen of the roads or Helen of the Hosts was the princess that appeared in a dream to Macsen Wledig and so bewitched the emperor that he left Rome to come to Britain and marry her. As with many other Celtic triple goddesses, transformed into Christian saints the three Helens were often combined and conflated in Welsh literary traditions.

In his *Histories of the Kings of Britain*, Geoffrey of Monmouth recounts how Helena the only daughter of King Coel of Colchester took over that kingdom after her father died of a grievous malady. The Roman senator Constantius who had been sent to Britain to keep the peace among the tribes married her and they had a son called Constantine. Eleven years later when his father died he took over as commander of the legions here. While still a youth, he marched on Rome and obtained the sovereignty of the whole world.

According to the account by Eusebius, Constantine was told in a dream on the eve of the battle at Mulvian Bridge to mark the chi-rho sign on his soldiers shields. In later versions he was directed in a vision before the campaign to add to the Christian monogram on his standard, the words 'conquer in this sign'. As emperor he granted freedom to all religions with special favour to Christians. In 323 under the chi-rho sign and the battle-cry 'God the highest Savour' he attacked and defeated his co-emperor Licinus. Constantine's father had been a devotee of Helios Apollo and one of the first gestures to the Christians as supreme emperor in 326 was the gift of the shrine of the Unconquered Sun in Nero's Circus, for the foundation of their new church to St Peter. When Christianity became the official religion of the Roman empire its centre was Byzantium, transformed and renamed as the City of Constantinople.

A temple on the Acropolis became a Christian church with a huge statue of the emperor. In its base it contained the sacred relics of Rome and in the orb-a symbol of world denomination – was embedded a fragment of the True Cross of Christ. Helena found the original cross on Golgotha, *place of skulls* and site of the Crucifixion. A sixteen-century poem by Wiliam Cynwal attributes the finding of the miracle-making blessed cross to her who recognised the true cross among the three on the hill. A second fragment was deposited there in the Church of the Holy Sepulchre and a third in Rome. In time splinters from the True Cross became the traditional gift of popes to proclaimed high kings and were usually encased and enshrined in precious ornaments in the churches dedicated to the Holy Cross.

Geoffrey later recounts the events around the arrival of Maximian, a Briton, who married the unnamed daughter of the dying king. After subduing the tribes, puffed up with pride and surquedry, he fitted out a mighty fleet and assembled every single armed warrior in Britain in order to subjugate the whole of Gaul. He was defeated by the Emperor Theodosius.

According to the *Life of Martin of Tours*, the saint was a close friend to Magnus Maximus and so he and his wife Elen were probably instructed by this dynamic man who is considered to have been the seminal influence on monasticism in Britain. When Elen returned to Britain, after his death in 388, with her sons Constantine and Peblig it was probably to the city of Ariconium within the kingdom of Archenfield. An entry in the Chronicles of Prosper of Aquitaine states that Constantine rose from the ranks of the military to despotism in Britain and crossed over to Gaul in 407. He was defeated and captured four years later at Arles bearing out St Jerome's comment, 'Britain the province fertile in producing tyrants'. Elen the mother of Peblig was commingled by later poets with Elen Luyddog as the mythical progenitress of the royal house of Dyfed. A tall stone called Carreg Faen Hir stood by Sarn Helen where it crossed Cefn Gelligaer with a dedication (now defaced) to Defrothi that may have referred to St Dyfrig who has many dedications in this area of south Herefordshire. He was also the founder of Llandaf, near the site of the Roman naval fort in Cardiff.

Sarn meaning causeway or track is usually thought of as an indication of a Roman road. But it could be a prehistoric trackway reused by the Romans, a medieval or even a later road. The combination of Helen associated with Sarn is considered by Richard Colyer to have been a corruption of *lleng*, legion, as in road used by the legion or even a corruption of *halen*, sea salt, since Sarn Helen runs from the sea to the sea with parts of it close to the wide sweep of Cardigan Bay.

The Dream of Macsen Wledig in the Mabinogion, is one of those remarkable dreams that we would now class in terms of lucid dreaming. It is as if the private imagining of the dreamer creates a chain reaction beyond the dream that is so powerful that the dreamer has to recreate the dream itself in order to find understanding, peace of mind or in the case of Macsen, his true love in person. The emperor of Rome lay down in the sun while out hunting and had a strange, haunting and unsettling dream. He had walked down the valley where he slept to the source of the river, climbed the highest mountain in the world and then was swept along a great river to a city. Over a bridge to a ship. Over the sea to an island where he saw a castle. Inside a maiden sat on a gold chair. She was the fairest that he had ever beheld and almost instantly they embraced. The emperor at that kiss awoke and from that moment on lost all pleasure in life.

Each day was a trial until he could sleep and meet again the dream maiden of his longing. He asked the wisest of his court who could not help him. He told the sages of Rome that he had a dream and in that dream was a maiden so fair that neither life nor spirit nor existence had any meaning for him. They in turn sent out messengers to all parts of the empire but to no avail. However one wise man suggested to the emperor that he return to the place where he first dreamt of the maiden so that messengers could retrace his steps. The messengers were able to follow his dream journey from Rome to the western edge of the empire and they found the castle on Anglesey. Helen told them that if their emperor loved her, he should come in person. He made the actual journey and then conquered Britain. When he came to Abersaint in Arfon he recognised the castle instantly. The girl he had dreamt was sitting in a chair of red gold. He embraced her and that night he slept with his dream maiden in person. For her bride price she asked for the island of Britain to be made safe with three strongholds. At *Y Gaer yn Arfon* – the original fort on the Hill of Llanbeblig where both were buried – to be called Segontium, at Caer Llion, at Caer Fyrddin or Moridunum and they should be connected with high roads. Subsequently known as Sarnau Helen, the roads of Elen of the hosts.

Roman Roads and Saintly Byways

There is a distinct lack of historical and archaeological evidence for any reliable sequence of the spread of Christianity into Wales up to the end of the fourth-century and even after the withdrawal of the legions. During the Constantine period with imperial backing for the new faith, a number of buildings with pagan shrines were constructed as at Lydney on the Severn in 364. Perhaps the popularity of the Nodens healing cult should be seen as part of a neo-Celtic revival among the Romanized ruling families, seemingly aware of the possible end of the empire. The old gods would be enshrined within the familiar urban model of bathhouses, offerings and dream divination. Whereas away from the towns and particularly among the tribes beyond the decaying network of roads and military forts, the religion of the people and the indigenous ritual cults would be cruder, closer to nature and their ancestral spirits. By the mid-five-hundreds, Gildas the Monk castigating the rulers of the Welsh kingdoms specifically mentions the twenty-four fawning bardic panegyrists of Maelgwn's court. The king had been (or educated as) a monk before returning 'to the old ways' of a Celtic overlord. Eventhough Maelgwn is usually portrayed in the *Lives* of many saints as a bogeyman, the subtext of the territorial disputes over church boundaries indicates the desire to legitimise the status of ecclesiastical sites. And to do so within an idealised religious society of that time. The Age of the Saints was almost five-hundred years earlier than many of the manuscripts that incorporated the folklore and popular tales of the saints.

The picture that emerges from the Roman period indicates that Christianity was an exotic religion among the many encouraged by the authorities. Mainly confined to the south-east and south-west of Britain and also around Hadrian's Wall and along the northern frontier. During the post-Roman period it gradually gained acceptance and a wider spread of influence. In many ways the early stone crosses are the only guide to general locations and the extent of the new faith throughout Wales. And, unlike what occurred in England after the onslaught of the Saxons and the Angles, scholarly opinion asserts that there was no break in the continuity of the church here, which was an episcopal type of Roman diocesan hierarchy. And there were monastic settlements for unspecified periods in the west but were still under the jurisdiction of a regional bishop rather than an abbot as was the case in Ireland.

The name of the present Welsh town Caerleon is derived from the Latin meaning the fort or camp of the legions. Sited as it was within a loop of the tidal river, the Romans called the military camp Isca from the Celtic term for water which is retained in the name of the river Usk. The changing form of the name is an indication of the continuity of use over the past two millennia and also that popular usage shows how the past devolves into the present. Excavations of this site has borne out its importance as one of the main military camps along the frontier zone.

Like Deva (Chester) in the north-east it was the centre of a series of linking roads and fortifications as far west as Moridunum (Carmarthen) which in turn was joined to Segontium (Caernarfon) by way of Sarn Helen. In fact the present road system of Wales is largely based on the Roman roads, defined as they were by geographical considerations and especially the north/south axis of communication but probably laid down on existing trackways wherever possible.

Nine miles to the east of Caerleon, Venta Silurum – the market town of the Silures – was built at Caerwent during the second-century. It had

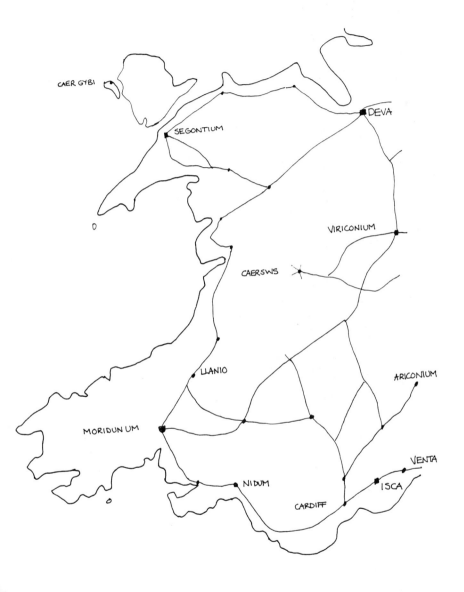

Roman roads and towns.

all the regular buildings of a Roman town and a temple with a private inner shrine and a sanctuary dedicated to a dual Romano-Celtic god. A stone head now in the National Museum in Cardiff may have come from a house shrine. The 'church' discovered by its excavator Nash-Williams was later deemed to be a cottage. The sole evidence of Christian activity was the graffiti scratch marks of a chi-rho symbol, on a fragment of a pewter bowl. It was found in 1906 in a sealed pottery urn set into the floor of a house opposite the basilica and dated to the fourth-century. The monogram was only identified in 1960. It may have been part of an *agape* set, used by the early Christians in what was then known as the fellowship of the table in honour of Christ's last supper. The Mass would take place in main room and when not used for this holy ritual the bowls for the bread and wine would be hidden in the floor beneath the table.

Outside the east gate of the town more than a hundred burials were discovered, some of which may have been Christian as laid out in the long-cist manner. A second cemetery inside the walls near the present church of St Tatheus revealed the same mixture of short and long-cist burials dated to the post-Roman period from the mid-fourth to the eighth-century. An Irish *Life* of the saint states that he set up his church here and in the *Life of Finnian*, that Cadog received his religious education from Tatheus before going to Lismore in Ireland.

The mixture of pagan and possible Christian burials has been found elsewhere in Wales as at Caer, Bayvil in Pembrokeshire. The latter was a pre-historic burial site and its continual use as late as the eighth-century shows one model of possible ecclesiastical development that ended in the early medieval period whereas the Roman cemetery continued to be incorporated into a later church. Such examples show the great gaps in our present knowledge and how much later in time than the fifth and sixth-century dates that are quoted, often in reputable publications, for the Christianization of the whole of Wales. This data could perhaps be seen as east-west burials being those of monks or ecclesiastics whereas the short-cist types for the ordinary people of the old and new religious faiths. After all Baptism was then the main rite which showed their adherence to Christ, and his image in the illuminated gospels was that of the resurrection in glory rather than the later mutilated Saviour figure.

It is only since archaeologists have been excavating in order to find material remains or sustainable structural evidence for the famed and fabulous settings from Welsh history that the premise of the literary claims for the 'Age of the Saints' and even of a Celtic church have begun to be seriously questioned.

After being ordained by Dubricius, who then marked out for Illtud the 'bounds of a burial place', the fame of Llanilltud Fawr (*Llantwit Major*) as 'the school of an illustrious Master of the Britons' attracted pupils like David, Samson and Paulinus who were in a sense the next generation of saints – now known only by their biblical names – and even Gildas who was said to have been a teacher there when he wrote his *De Excidio Brittaniae*. However excavations around the present churchyard failed to reveal any evidence for this most important of all the Celtic sites in Wales. The earliest church buildings found were post-Norman. This is not to say that the original enclosure which may have been modest in its extent was not located somewhere else in the same area, for the Normans had their own grandiose ideas of where and how churches should be located.

A conference on 'Christianity in Britain 300-700' was held at the University of Nottingham in 1967 which brought together the range of current thinking on the available historical, theological and material evidence. In 1975, Kathleen Hughes gave the O'Donnell lecture in Oxford entitled – The Celtic Church: Is this a valid concept? The issues she raised in this seminal essay were brought out in depth and detail at an archaeological conference in Cardiff in 1991 which had the same question mark after the Celtic Church. Unsurprisingly the editors in their summing-up of the papers published from this gathering stated that it was in archaeology where the evidence for the ecclesiastical landscape was growing and when used in conjunction with historical and other sources may improve our understanding of the period. The contribution of aerial photography in surveying the 'llan' church enclosures was an important advance here. In fact the Roman road to Carmarthen was recently revealed to have an extension westwards as far as Whitland. However without a spectacular site-find that might extend current perspectives as occurred with the Sutton Hoo royal burials in East Anglia, the St Ninian's Isle hoard in Shetland and the Derrynaflan hoard of liturgical metalwork in Ireland, then the picture of Christian Wales as an impoverished, inward-looking backwater persists.

The present east-west road through the Vale of Glamorgan follows the Roman road to Loughar camp above Llanrhidian Sands. The villas at Llanilltud Fawr and Merthyr Mawr were probably connected by some kind of track and to the main roadway. Roads from present-day Neath and Cardiff went northwards towards Brecon Gaer. The trackways through the upland areas appeared not to have been in use then but later during the early Christian period. More than a dozen have been postulated that divide into two broad groups – on the west up to Landovery and on the east to Brecon and Bronllys.

As with the Roman roads proper there are a number of church sites and inscribed stones that are associated with the trackways but whether this constitutes sufficient evidence for the eastward spread of Christianity into Wales is an open question. Especially as the actual evidence for the use of the Roman roads specifically in the promulgation of the new faith is so sketchy. The only buildings that have been dated to the early Christian period are the Dinas Powys post-built timber hall and the post-holes of a church? beneath the present ruin on Burry Holms. Both sites

BURRY HOLMS

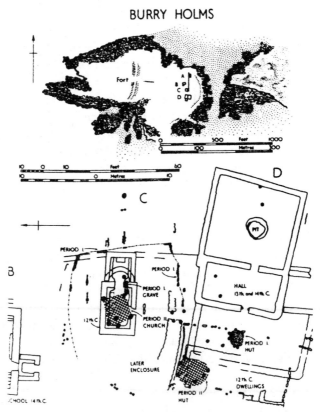

Excavations at Burry Holms. Crown Copyright: R.C.A.H.M.W.

are on the south-western coast. Nash-Williams pointed out the lack of early inscribed stones in the south-eastern corner of Wales. He was also of the opinion that contrary to the general idea of nameless Christian refugees fleeing from the turmoil of the Roman mainland, Christianity was introduced into Wales and Ireland through the western seaways as a deliberate policy by the church in Gaul.

It is also suggested that when monasticism developed in Wales it remained within the established system of regional bishoprics whereas in Ireland it forged a new relationship based on the paruchiae or mother houses ruled by an abbot within the family kin of the founder-saint. Bishops did not lose their importance within the liturgical organisation of the priesthood but only their supreme authority modelled on the hierarchical Roman system of governing was bypassed. According to K. Hughes it was the Welsh kings who exercised patronage and supported the role of the bishop whereas in Ireland it was the leaders of the kin or extended tribal families who held power. They granted land for monasteries but it effectively remained within their kin. In time separate laws were enacted that enabled the church to become an independent body and embrace once more the diocesan system that Patrick had introduced there.

From the evidence in the *Book of Llandaff*, the monasticism of its founders was included in so far as it would strengthen the claims of the bishops of Llandaf to the churches and lands dedicated to them. The manuscript included the *Lives* of Dyfrig, Teilo and Euddogwy, and charters that were made out to them and 'to their successors in the see of Llandaf'. Canon Doble summed-up the circumstances surrounding the *Liber Landavensis*. Dyfrig was the chief saint of 'Herefordshire with many church dedications there and Teilo's are mainly throughout South Wales whereas the third has only one place which bears his name and he therefore must be a later bishop.

While scholars admit that such charters are mainly fraudulent they still pick through them for nuggets that might illuminate the past. W. Davies and J.W. James believe they are based on genuine records and that the internal chronology and dating can be established. K. Hughes thought that some documentation was drawn upon and by isolating the properties claimed by individual bishops she drew up a series of distribution maps that showed restricted patterns of dedications. This suggested the maintenance of a territorial diocese that was more influenced by the Romano-British church than the Celtic elements introduced during the early medieval period.

According to the eighth-century *Life,* Samson as a boy was educated at Llanilltud Fawr and at his ordination by Dubricius as deacon and later as a priest, a dove hovered above his head on both occasions. At Ynys Byr – probably Caldey Island off the south Pembrokeshire coast – he continued his austere life of prayer and work. On the way to visit his sick father he had a curious encounter in a wood with one of the aboriginal inhabitants of Demetia. The young deacon who was leading his horse fled at the sight of the hag with wild grey hair and red rags. She ran after him throwing a boarspear but the young man had already fainted in fright. Samson questioned the old woman who told him that she was alone in the wood but her mother and eight sisters lived nearby. Since she was unable or unwilling to heal the deacon or 'do any good', Samson cursed her. As the story relates she fell down on the left side and expired on the spot. When he returned to Ynys Byr with his father and uncle who had decided to devote themselves to the religious life, Samson was questioned (presumably by Dubricius) as to whether he had knocked her on the head with a stone or actually killed her with a saint's curse. As it was the latter and since the deacon was out cold at the time her death occurred, his account was accepted. He was then appointed as abbot of the monastery. Pirus who was 'an illustrious and holy priest' was understandably upset at being demoted. It seemed that the Irishman had taken more than a passing fancy to the mead cask and got so inebriated that he fell into the wellshaft. The monks heard him shouting and pulled him out but he died later that night.

Apart from the inclusion of two archetypes – the Irish drunkard and the witch who cannot heal – the anecdote is noteworthy in that it shows the authority of St Dubricius (Dubric or Dyfrig in modern Welsh) as bishop at two very different Celtic monastic sites. At Llanilltud Fawr in the Vale of Glamorgan and on the island hermitage, each ruled by an abbot. In fact the reason that Samson left the former was because Illtud's two nephews were jealous of his pre-eminence and feared that he would deprive them of a 'hereditary worldly possession'. Caldey island is opposite Penally where Teilo was born and in one of the charters attached to the *Liber Llandavensis,* its church was granted to Dyfrig.

Samson's family had divided up their possessions into three parts – one retained, one for the poor and one for the foundation of a monastery, no doubt dedicated to Samson himself. However when his mother Anna asks him to consecrate the churches so founded, he demured because he had not yet been made bishop (of Dol in Brittany). A common link between many Welsh saints is that they are related to ruling kin-groups so perhaps such family foundations were more common than the present evidence suggests.

The distribution patterns of church dedications to British saints in Wales are generally local, almost all regional. For instance those to David are in the south-west with none in the north. Eventhough the main centres of Cadog and Illtud in the Vale of Glamorgan seem to have been based on the Celtic mode, dedications to the former appear to be more extensive clustered about Llancarfan and eastwards in Gwent along the Roman road. Cadoc is one of the few early saints who has been directly linked to the church of St Tatheus in Caerleon. He was educated here by the Irish hermit, also known as Meuthius and at Lismore in Ireland before returning home. The reason given in the *Life* was that Bachan, a Latin teacher from Italy had recently arrived within 'those borders' and Cadog and his followers wished to become pupils.

Given the above outline of information, one can understand the need of historians to opt for a restrictive viewpoint rather than the expansive Celtic church with its very unhistorical but massive hagiography. They would probably paint the same picture for Ireland if the evidence for the contrary was not so overwhelming. However the core questions remain of when, how and where Christianity, like the later phase of monasticism, developed.

Whatever the motives behind the formulation of the *Book of Llandaff*, the fact is that it was written at a period when the Welsh church in the south-east was clearly in an expansive phase. Likewise in the west, the Life of David and illuminated manuscripts were being produced at Llanbadarn Fawr. The decorative high crosses of this period were another sign of this confidence. Stylistically the stone crosses may have been derivative but the amalgamation of outside influences is one of the great traditions of Celtic art from its very beginnings in continental Europe. There is a definite quality about the sculpting of the abstract motifs and patterns in such high crosses as in Nevern churchyard that is very different from those in Ireland, England and Scotland, that can safely be described as Welshness. Perhaps the high crosses at Coychurch and Llandough in the Vale of Glamorgan that are usually thought of as

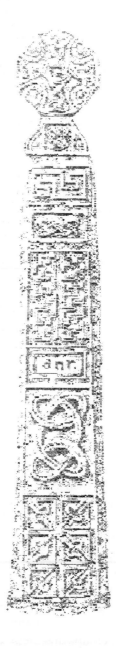

Nevern Cross, Pembrokeshire.

24

excessive examples of stylisation done at the end of the Celtic period, may also be seen in the light of this confidence. And at a time when such expansiveness would soon be overwhelmed by the arrival of the Normans.

St Teilo and the Seven Watermen

Sometime about the middle of the ninth-century the illuminated gospel-book of Saint Chad had lain 'on the altar of Teilo' at Llandeilo Fawr in Carmarthenshire. It probably was penned in Ireland a century or so earlier but there are a number of entries written in Welsh and Latin in the margins that state it was a gift from God and offered onto the altar of the saint. Three important named people and the monks described as 'the whole family of Teilo' witnessed the gift. There is no information about the saint nor how the book itself came to Wales. However it does indicate that Llandeilo Fawr was an important ecclesiastical centre then and that its founder was still highly venerated centuries after his death. The manuscript may have found its way into England as a gift from Hywel Dda to Athelstan, king of Wessex and Mercia, in 943. It was later donated to St Chad's church at Lichfield, hence its name and present location.

In the *Book of Llandaff* we learn that the saint was called Eliud, a corruption of his birthname Elios (sun) from the Greek helios and was born at Penalun (Penally in Pembrokeshire) who claimed the body after his death. The Triads commemorate the miracle of the triplication of Teilo's body which God created for the first to be at Llandaf, the second at Llandeilo Fawr and the third in Penalun. In the *Life of Oudoceus* is an encounter with him being accosted at Cydweli by 'some covetous and disaffected people' who accuse him of carrying off the treasures of Saints David and Teilo. The assailants were struck blind and their spear-arms paralysed. However, when they repented they were healed by his prayers.

This may have been a reference to the relics of Teilo being brought to Llandaf. The building of the present cathedral at Cardiff was started by the Norman bishop Urban in 1120 who reclaimed the bones of Dyfrig from the island of Bardsey. The tombs of both founders became an important asset as the focus for medieval pilgrimage and explains the collating of the *Lives* of these three saints in the *Liber Landavensis* as part of an agenda to make Llandaf the main episcopal centre of Wales at that time.

In 1870 a small Celtic cross was discovered embedded in the back wall of a shed over St Teilo's well in the Bishop's Palace. It was also known as the Dairy Well from the story of Oudoceus returning from his harrowing journey and feeling thirsty, walked to the holy well on the steep slope above the church. There were women washing butter. He asked if any had a drinking vessel and when the women replied that they had nothing except the butter in their hands he took some and shaped it into the form of a bell and drank from it. It was at once changed into a metal bell. This may have been the Teilo bell that in another version of his *Life* had the power to heal the sick, to revive the blind and make the deaf hear.

There is a more famous well dedicated to the saint in the parish of Maenclochog in Pembrokeshire in which a human skull known as *Penglog Teilo* was used to imbibe the holy water. Apparently a large flat ringing stone stood nearby and when struck would reverberate loudly as the well water was carried in the skull into the church of Llandeilo. It was broken up because the noise frightened the horses! The use of the cranium cap – dark in colour and polished from continuous handling – as a cup for the holy water was essential to a cure. There is a story of a man with his sick son who on getting back home to Swansea returned immediately to the well because the boy had not drunk from *St Teilo's skull*. For centuries the traditional guardians of the skull were a family named Melchior who owned the land around the well. However, when the skull was sold or otherwise given away the family was plagued by misfortune. The well has been capped and like the ruined church, has only the stone foundations still standing.

Two inscribed stones now in Maenclochog church came from Llandeilo. Recently another stone with a ring-cross was discovered not far away at a ruined Chapel as forming a lintel over another well used as a baptistery. Above the cross as originally set upright is a rare Christian symbol of a fish, incised by two intersecting arcs.

Fish was the only food eaten by the seven watermen of Llandyfrgwyr. As seven fish would be provided for them daily and left on a stone, it came to be known as Llech Myneich, or the monk's stone. Perhaps this is the very stone from which the story originated. In the *Liber Landavensis* it accounts for the name of the church in the land grant claimed as part of Teilo's holdings. A poor couple whose poverty was increased every year by the birth of a son asked the saint for advise. He said they should refrain from intercourse for seven years. This they did but thereafter when they resumed their conjugal pleasure, the women eventually gave birth to seven sons all at once. Her husband had enough and was trying to drown them in the river Taf when Teilo intervened, rescued the boys and took them to be brought up at Llandeilo. As the boys were called *dyfrgwyr* (watermen) and eat only fish the church was thereafter known as Llandyfrgwyr or Llanddowror, the Monastery of the Watermen. The seven brothers later studied under Dyfrig who sent them to Mathry where the church is dedicated to the Seven Holy Martyrs. From here they went to Cenarth on the river Teifi.

In the churchyard above the falls, still famous for its salmon fishing from skin coracles, is an Ogam inscribed stone which curiously enough was brought here from Maenclochog church. All three Ogam inscribed stones, once located at Llandeilo may commemorate three generations of Irish chieftains – Curcagnus, the son of Andegellus; Andegellus the son of Cavetus; and Coimagnus the son of Cavetus. The name Andegellus is inscribed in Latin and Ogam letters with a linear cross of cross-crosslet

Inscribed stone from Llandeilo, Pembrokeshire.

27

type, thought to be contemporary and dated to the sixth-century. The Voteporix inscription stone with a simple ring-cross also dated to the same period was found at Castell Dwyran which is about five miles away and indicates a strong Irish presence in this area with some of the earliest Christian communities located at Llandeilo and Llandysilio on both sides of the eastern Cleddau.

Mathry is unusually located on a prominent hill. In the church is a Latin and Ogam inscribed stone with a ringed cross and two later cross stones are set in the wall outside that came from Rhoslanog which has a tradition of being an early burial ground. The western Cleddau river passes below Mathry. Llanddowror is on a tributary to the Taf at the eastern side of the peninsula and Cenarth is on the river Teifi to the north-east. If one adds Nevern and Llandudoch, the area so defined includes the highest concentration of early Christian sites and Ogam inscribed stones in south-west Wales.

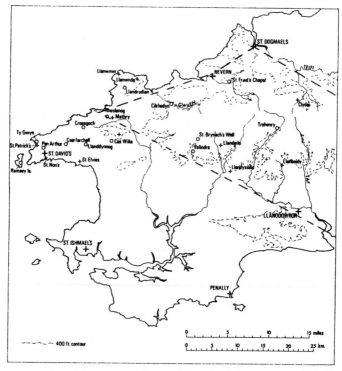

Area of Early Christian sites and Ogam stones in north-east Pembrokeshire.
(After J.M. Lewis).

It would seem that by the time of the Llandaf *Lives*, mingling oral traditions and property rights of the saints' monasteries within the framework of a founder-figure, any traditions of Irish saints of the sixth-century and later had died out or were ignored. The process of rededication of churches and relocation of saints' cults was common. The beginnings of Christianity in Wales was entwined within the Roman system of centralised control but in the post-Roman era it had to come to terms with regional tribal Celtic culture. And with the inroads of the Irish from the west, the Brythons from the north and later Anglo-Saxons from the east, each group brought their traditions, their language, their religion and religious rituals.

From the material evidence and distribution of the inscribed stone crosses one suspects that the Irish and British incomers were Christian. Later the effects of the localization of saints dedications from eponymous ancestors such as Ceredig in Ceredigion tended to obscure any Irish legacy south of the river Ystwyth. As the sons of Cunedda who were said to have driven the Irish raiders from Anglesey pushed southwards the older cult of St Finnian was masked as Welsh 'under the Brythonic forms of his name as Finnianus whence Finnio' and the 'new' saints names invariably included the element *gwyn*, fair, corresponding to *find* in Irish.

There are various references in Welsh poetry to the seven blessed cousins; to the seven saints who broke the stone 'an awful roundness'; to the seven who went to Rome to pray for rain after three years of drought, named as St's Dewi, Cybi, Seiriol, Deiniol, Bruno, Cadfach and Cynfarch. Yet another reference is to the fact that the seven saw 'the star' which may refer to the Pleiades group but more probably to the Star of Bethlehem as the seven harbingers of Christianity here. There are also a number of dedications in Ireland to the Church of the Seven (Tory Island and the Aran Islands) and an account in the *Life* of Declan of Ardmore that may make the reference clearer.

Here it was the seven aged saints at Ardmore who took up the young deacon. Foretelling that one day he would be bishop and that they would give themselves and their land for churches to him. These seven saints witnessed a heavenly ball of fire rising from the roof of the church at Meg Sceith, near Lismore, with angels singing sweet psalms and ascending upwards to heaven. It was at Lismore, on the bend of the river Blackwater, that Cadog was educated before returning to Wales.

The cryptic reference to the seven indicated that their old churchlands

– some may even have been established during the pre-Patrician period in South Munster – should henceforth be under the guidance of St Declan of the Deisi, the same tribal group who settled in south-west Wales. And the coastal setting of the medieval monastery of Ardmore in Co. Waterford with its tall round tower, ornate stone churches, Romanesque stone carving, holy well and saints relics certainly represented, as Llandaf did around the same period, a new phase of Christian expansion.

The Irish Sea Province

A land area roughly comprising the hinterlands of western Britain, Brittany and east to south Ireland has been called the southern zone. The northern one was centred on the Isle of Man. Visible from here are its four high points – Snowdon in north Wales, Mountains of Mourne in Northern Ireland, Scafell in Cumbria and the hills of Galloway. The low lying areas extended to the Hebrides. The notion of a maritime province helped focus on the cultural influences and social interactions of the ancient peoples who inhabited this region bordering the Irish Sea and St George's Channel. The term itself came into prominence in the work of Professor E.G. Bowen of Aberystwyth, especially his books on the early saints and western seaways. A conference on the history and archaeology of the Irish Sea Province was published in 1970.

Since the Stone Age cross-cultural influences in the forms of stone axes and pottery vessels; in the architecture of megalithic monuments; rock art in the passage tombs; and in designs of Bronze Age artifacts found on both shores of the Irish Sea. However the archaeological record is mute on the language or identity of the people who used them. The activities of the Iron Age Celtic peoples broadened the general picture but it is from the post-Roman period onwards that a maritime province could begin to be considered a homogenous cultural entity with common language, society and religion. The P-Celtic and Q-Celtic spoken in Wales and Ireland were well established. Loan words from the Latin liturgy are evident in both countries with a shift from Britain westwards that mirrored the spread of early Christianity. The linguistic inroads eastwards are found in the use of the Irish word *cnoc* for hills in south-west Wales and particularly in the Ogam form of writing on the early Christian stone monuments that are particularly concentrated from north

Pembrokeshire to the Brecon Beacons.

Irish tribal communities of this time settled along the length of western Britain. Historically attested groups were the Dal Riata in Argyll, the Laigin and Deisi in Wales, and perhaps in Somerset and Cornwall. The latter do not appear to have left historical traces although the establishment of monastic centres at Glastonbury, Malmesbury and even in Dorset might well suggest some link with the earlier migrants. The Dalriadians, on the other hand, became so well established that they formed a regional kinship to eventually provide the first royal king in tenth-century Scotland. The Iona community under Columba from 560 onwards was religiously affiliated with its social and political aspirations.

During the next century the spread of Irish Christianity in its formal aspects under an abbot and conservative Easter calendar, both distinct from the new Roman orthodoxy, was finally curtailed at the Synod of Whitby in 663. The monastery here and those at Lindesfarne and Melrose continued under the Anglo-Saxons. The artistic legacy of the illuminated manuscripts, fine metalwork and stone carving that resulted from the cultural fusion in Northumbria influenced both the development of Pictish and Irish religious art in all these forms.

The earlier expansion of the Angles up the spine of Britain overran many of the established Celtic kingdoms and forced the Votadini or the Gododdin of lowland Scotland near Edinburgh to migrate southwards to the relative safety of north Wales. The reference to this legendary move are problematic as it may have begun earlier under Maximus to protect Segontium against possible Irish attack when he took the legions and the British to Gaul. So whether they walked overland in large contingents or many smaller groups in boats by way of Man as has been suggested, is entirely speculative.

In fact, with the notable exception of Samson, Teilo and Cybi travelling by boat, the *Lives* of the Celtic saints are particularly non-informative as to how they travelled to their so called missionary activity in Wales, Brittany and Ireland. However, Brynach crossed the Milfordhaven on a stone and Illtud saw a stone sargophous miraculously crossing the sea towards his cell. The Irish saint Brigid was said to have crossed the seas to Anglesey on a sod of grass.

Bowen, quoting the remark by Nora Chadwick that the early church was one of seafarers and that communication by sea then was easier and quicker than by land, postulated a series of well-travelled sea lanes across

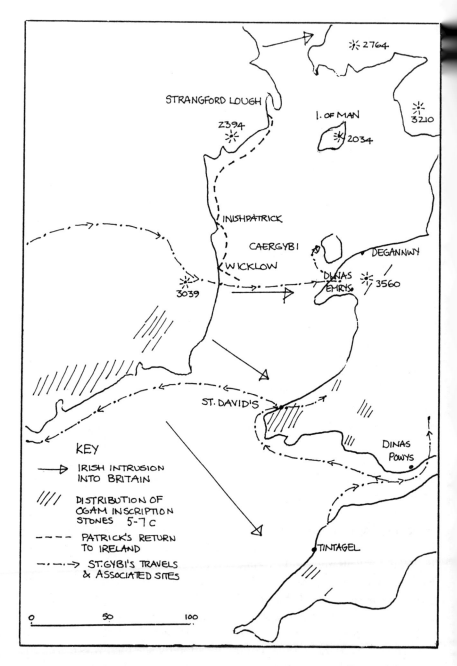

5th to 7th century cultural movements across the Irish Sea province.

the Irish 'pond', supplemented by short coastal hopping and trans-peninsula tracks to avoid the dangerous headlands. Cybi in his 'planked boat' used the most direct crossing from Wicklow to Penrhyn Llŷn and then walked inland for a few miles to the holy well known as Ffynnon Cybi Sant. He finally ended up building his church, Caergybi, in the Roman fort at Holyhead on Anglesey that was given him by Maelgwn Gwynedd.

Years earlier when he had left Wales for Ireland he appears to have used the southern short crossing from St David's Head. However since he studied with Enda on Aran Mor in Galway Bay he may sailed around the south-west coast. The emphasis on his wooden boat could be to point up the difference between it and the more usual sea going Irish currachs.

In fact, given that he was a Cornish prince who had initially travelled across the Bristol Channel to south Wales and a boat builder, perhaps he was master of the boat as well as religious leader of his family of monks. The stratified Celtic society of this period meant that only those who were born into sailing families; or who belonged to the 'professional' class of poet, lawmaker, monk and priest; or who were closely related to the ruling kin groups; could travel individually. This makes Patrick's own account of his escape from slavery in Ireland all the more remarkable.

His *Confessio* is one of the few documents extant from this period. Written according to the experts in sixth-century Latin and by a man who was not a scholar but conversant with the common range of the writings of the Church Fathers. It records his spiritual path from a youth looking after cattle on the mountains in the north, the doubts about his calling, the slights and snide treatment by the church elders in Britain, to the summation of his mission as a bishop bringing the true faith to the Irish. Traditionally he is supposed to have arrived in 432 and by the time he died an old man had converted the whole Ireland to Christianity. Recent scholarship confines his mission to the north and west provinces during the later part of the fifth-century.

The exact location of his early home is unknown, thought by some to have been Galloway or near the Antoninus Wall. North Wales and even the Bristol Channel have been postulated. What is certain is that his family had social standing in a Romano-British milieu. Grandson of a priest with a father who was an official and church deacon, the sixteen-year old was captured by Irish pirates and taken to a beach along with many others before sailing across to Ireland. This was not a rare occurrence for he mentions that 'many thousands' like himself had been taken into slavery by the Irish, living a life so different from the comfortable villa surroundings in which he had been accustomed.

Tending cattle on a mountain side in all weathers for six years whether on Slemish in Antrim or at Killala in Mayo as Tirechan, his second biographer claims, he turned to constant prayer as his only solace. Patrick writes that he heard in a dream that he would be soon depart to his homeland and an angel, Victoricus the messenger, appeared to him and told him that his ship was ready.

There is no mistaking the biblical tone here nor the prophetic dream that induced him to walk the two-hundred miles to a harbour that he had never been to before and actually see a ship that was ready to set sail. However, the steersman refused to let him on board.

Later one of the crew shouted at him to join them. The port is likely to have been somewhere in the south. The sea-journey lasted three whole days. He mentions the crew and a party with whom he walked across a wild uninhabited country for twenty-eight days, so the boat must have been a sizeable one making the crossing to what could be Brittany. A large planked type that the Veneti traders from this region had used against the Romans in their unfortunate sea-battle against Julius Caesar. He subsequently caused a mass migration into Britain of the tribes known as the Dumnonii who settled in Devon and along the river Severn. It appears that these were the same peoples who returned to their homeland of Armorica 'the land by the sea' during the Age of the Saints hence the close correspondences between Welsh, Cornish and Breton languages from this period.

It was on this journey that the saint had his second dream. More like a nightmare, for it felt as if a dark weight of a huge rock fell and enveloped him which he thought was the devil and woke up shouting helias, helias! The third dream was of the letter-carrier with a bundle of letters. One was addressed to the 'holy boy', signed on the cover and as he read it he could hear the sweet voices of the Irish inviting him to come and visit them.

Muirchu states that Patrick spent many years in Gaul at Auxerre under Bishop Germanus, receiving minor orders before returning to his parent's home where he had his third vision. By now it had been transformed into an angel bringing the summons as the Irish were crying out for him to return there and 'walk again among us'. He then began his mission which was said to have lasted thirty years. Using the money from his estate in Britain, he paid a retinue of the sons of the chieftains, according to local custom, as well as giving presents to the chiefs and paying the law-makers. This may have been a reference to the custom of fosterage of the young that occurred at all levels of Celtic society in Ireland. The giving and receiving of such gifts may have been one reason why he was later censured by his ecclesiastical elders in Britain. Both biographers tell of the 'books' and other religious or liturgical objects he brought with him as well as employing artisans to make them. His ship which was laden with 'religious treasures' landed in the estuary of the Vartry River in Co. Wicklow. He decided to visit his old master and sailed northwards stopping at a small island, Inispatrick near Dublin, before arriving at Strangford Lough. The party stopped at the mouth of the Slaney river and hid the boat before walking inland. This remark may reflect the practice of the seventh-century when monks travelled extensively along the river valleys where many of the important monastic centres were located but it also shows that the crew were part of Patrick's entourage.

Dates like Patrick arriving in Ireland in 432 or the expulsion of Colm Cille (Columba) to Scotland in 563 and the Synod at Whitby in 664 have become pivotal turning points in relating the story of Christianity in Ireland and its revival in Britain. In establishing a history of beginnings the tendency is to ignore the extremely ancient religious practices of pre-history that the Christian-Judaic sects displaced as well as other turning points of the early period we can still term the Dark Ages. For instance, the collapse of the empire with the closing down of the road system from the frontiers, may have left behind 'urbanized' interracial and multi-caste townships around the old forts, especially along the Hadrian's Wall where communities, including Christians, would be vulnerable to the slave-traders now supplying Ireland rather than Rome.

The incursions of the Franks and the Visigoths caused an exodus of refugees from Gaul using the western seaways to find refuge and subsequently opened up new markets (to use the modern jargon) here in wine, beads and pottery. Supplying not only the established chiefdoms of Dinas Powys and Tintagel but probably also some smaller Christian communities spreading along the coasts. A particular form of early cross slab with or without a cross symbol and a single name inscribed with the final I horizontal to the rest of the letters, found in Cornwall, Wales and on the Isle of Man may indicate this intrusion. Along with two examples now in St Nicholas Church near Strumble Head in Pembrokeshire, is a slab with neat Roman lettering around an equal-armed cross.

The epidemic known as the yellow plague was another important pivot. It became a central factor in many of the *Lives* of the Celtic saints and was probably the main impetus for the particular Celtic form of monasticism that swept Ireland in the mid-sixth-century. It led to the repopulation of 'Little Britain' by the descendants of those who had migrated here nearly five hundred years previously. This was the period when the southern area of the maritime province came into its own enclosing the seas almost like an inland lake.

Under the year 547 the Welsh Chronicles recorded 'a great mortality in which died Maelgwn, king of north Wales *The Annales Cambriae* set down events and happenings between the fifth and tenth-century although first composed sometime around the middle of those years. The writer of the *Life* of St Teilo described some of the effects and why it was called the *yellow pestilence*. It made all the people who were seized by it, to be yellow and without blood.

Furthermore if anyone tried to apply a remedy to the sick person, not only had the medicine no effect but the disease brought both to death. It 'seized Maelgwn and destroyed his country'. It was likened to a column of a watery cloud sweeping over the ground like a rain cloud. A similar description can be found in Adamnan's *Life* of Saint Columba of a rain cloud which dropped a pestiferous rain on Ireland that caused festering sores on people's bodies and on the udders of animals.

When Teilo returned from his pilgrimage to Rome, with David and Padarn, he is said to have had to flee to Brittany in order to avoid the yellow plague. This seemed to be the universal way of dealing with such epidemics, getting as far away as possible although the earliest recording of one in the *Annales Cambriae*, for the year 526, had Saint Briog journeying from there to Llandyfriög in Ceredigion in answer to the plea of the inhabitants as their last remaining hope of 'escaping so great a peril'. The Irish *Annals* state that a great mortality prevailed in Ireland this year (547) which was called *buidhe conail* (yellow plague) and a great number of the saints died of it.

When news that the yellow pestilence had ceased in Britain, after seven years and seven months, Teilo sent messengers to gather together the scattered exiles in France and Italy 'and wherever they had gone' in order that they might all return home and 'he prepared three very large ships to transport them across the channel'.

It is probably no coincidence that from this period of the early saints with the ideal of the great overland pilgrimage to Rome and Jerusalem, that the epidemics began to occur of such magnitude as would be recorded then. Causes that we might now deem important to the spread of disease such as foreign contact, unaccustomed food in hotter climates and the overcrowding typical of monastic settlements on the pilgrimage routes were considered, if at all, as unavoidable and commonplace. The epidemic known as the yellow plague was the first of many such pestilences recorded with ever-recurring frequency in Britain during the following centuries.

A number of historians have commented on the yellow plague as a catalyst of change during this time. Liam de Paor is of the opinion that it was the crucial contribution to the growth of Irish monasticism. To those holy men who were advocating self-discipline and mortification of the body, the plague might have seemed heaven-sent, showing in unmistakable physical detail the sins of the flesh. A divine rebuke to older churchmen and women that their worldly concerns were misplaced and that intense prayer and severe penance was the message of the dying Christ. In many ways it was the first real test of faith for those in the west who had probably become Christians through repetitive prayers, psalm singing and learning the gospel stories by rote. The idea of Original Sin, so central to the new Christian doctrine and so alien to the Celtic soul, could now be illustrated by the liverish flesh of people everywhere. On the other hand for those who held firm to their ancient religion the gods of the land and the skies were showing their displeasure in no uncertain terms.

Another factor which is not often taken into account is the cyclic change of weather patterns. The cold and wet towards the end of the Roman era may have caused some population shifts from the uplands. In West Wales it may have led to the final abandonment of the large hill forts. As the weather improved so tribes began to expand once more and groups like the Deisi were moved from their traditional homelands and forced to cross the Irish Sea. From the evidence in the Dyfed genealogies, the location of the Group 1 inscribed Christian stones and place-names, their settlements inland across Demetia and then in Brecon has been postulated. The dynasty of Brycheiniog appears to have gained control of

Dyfed by the sixth-century and facilitated the spread of the saintly clan known as the 'Children of Brychan' westwards across Wales. Saint Brynach has a group of dedications at both extremes and the *Life of Carantoc* refers to an Irish invasion of Ceredigion when the saint was a young man. Later, perhaps under the threat of the oncoming plague, the 'Children' moved south-westwards into Cornwall and Brittany and even to south-east Ireland. The monastery of St Cynog – one of the sons of Brychan – at Merthyr Cynog in Breconshire may have been the centre of this original migration.

The Goidelic settlement in south Wales spans a period from either the early or late fifth to the late seventh-century which makes the plague of the mid-five-hundreds a watershed in their influence on the spread of Christianity. If one takes the accounts of the plague and its seven years duration from the life of St Teilo as a broadly accurate picture of the period, then the Brythonic peoples from south-east Wales were also part of this movement. Very little is known about Celtic medicine of the time but it seems to have had two basic approaches to disease. One was nursing, real care and attention for the patients, using herbs and unlimited rest as a cure and the other was to get as far as possible from an epidemic. For those now drawn to the Christian life, this movement was an ideal opportunity to seek out a lonely or 'desert place' in which to live their lives in prayer and meditation. The fact of repetitive references to such events as recorded in manuscripts over centuries should not lead to an inference that a major movement of people took as long as the memory of it. The Potato Famine of just a century and a half ago is thought to have caused four million people in Ireland to perish or migrate in just so many years.

Perhaps the old Roman towns and roadways were only instrumental in the spread of Christianity in so far as they were seen as the epicentre of the most fearful plague to decimate the peoples of the Celtic west. One result of it was the use of the western seaways as an escape route and as the main avenue for the re-introduction of the Christian faith into West Wales.

The Men from the North

Native historians presented Wales as a land of beleagured kingdoms. Periodically fighting among themselves as much as against the Anglo-Saxons, Normans and English. They tended to view Irish intrusion after the Romans as short lived and without lasting influence eventhough place-names and the genaelogy of the Dyfed kings indicated many settled generations there. Nennius had ascribed the formation of Gwynedd, the most powerful kingdom to emerge from the Dark Ages, to its founder Cunedda whose sons 'expelled' the Irish before settling in the mountainous region around Snowdonia. The dates of the alleged transmigration of the Gododdin from the Lothians, south of the Firth of Forth, has been variously argued from the late 300's to the late 600's. The concern here is whether or not they were Christian before they left and did they take their saints and holymen with them? Or perhaps followed on later! Like Columba and his monks nearly fifty years after the Irish had settled Dal Riata on the west coast of Scotland.

In the area south of the Forth which approximates to the homelands they left, hundreds of longcist burials were found to be clustered in large open cemeteries. Such cemeteries appear to have been common elsewhere in Southern Scotland near the east coast around St Andrews and in North Berwick. The grave coffins were made of a long stone sided 'box' with slabs on top and were then laid out in rows side by side. The body was interred with the head pointing to the west or south-west, without ornament or grave-goods. It was the combination of these three factors that led the first of such excavations at Kirkliston, near Edinburgh, over a century ago, to be described as Christian burials. The fact that the cemetery was near an inscribed monument known as the Catstane clinched the association. The recent excavation at the Catstane has revealed a more irregular arrangement around the stone itself as distinct from the hundreds of burials in rows. Modern archaeologists are much more cautious in their attribution of such wholesale Christian burials for a number of complex reasons but the most disturbing one is the lack of any evidence on the ground for churches or chapels. Use of air photography has clearly demonstrated this except where the cemetery itself is a late ninth-century foundation.

The heroes of the poem Gododdin (attributed to Aneirin) defeated at Catterick were presented as Christian warlords attempting to stem the tide of the heathen Angles moving north into their homelands.

'The warriors arose; they assembled;
Together, with one accord, they attacked.
Short were their lives,
Long their kinsmens' grief for them.'

A late medieval *Life of Kentigarn* by Jocelyn states that the saint, who was born of the royal house of Gododdin, was called back to Strathclyde by Rhydderch Hen, after a lengthy stay in Wales. The king, who according to Adamnan had been baptised in Ireland, defeated the pagan forces at the battle of Arderydd in 573. Edinburgh did not fall to the English until fifty years later but the powerful stronghold of Dumbarton in Strathclyde may have helped preserve both religious and the literary material that included the poems of Taliesin, the exploits of Arthur and Merlin going mad after the above battle. The circumstances that brought it into Wales many centuries later are not known but it formed one of the great story-telling traditions of the Middle Ages.

Tradition associates Kentigarn with a number of foundations in Wales but the most famous was the monastery of Llanelwy (Flint) in the old cantref of Rhos. It eventually bore the name of his disciple St Asaph when a bishopric was founded there in 1143. A legend attached to the place concerns the older saint who after a night of prayer standing with arms outstretched in a stream during winter, was so cold that he became rigid. The boy was sent to get some heat and returned with live coals in his apron. A dialogue between the two maintained that it was the Asa's innocence that enabled him to perform this miracle whereas the boy countered that it was due to the holiness of the saint himself. When Kentigarn left he took two-thirds of the 965 monks, leaving Asa or Asaph in charge. It seems to have been a conceit about recording the exact number as the 20,000 saints on Bardsey and the 1,200 monks to there from Bangor-is-y-coed monastery after the other half were slain. When the church at Llangyndeyrn in Carmarthenshire – also dedicated to Kentigarn – was being restored, 497 adult skeletons were found in five layers deep and closely packed together. As there were no wounds on the bodies that all appeared to have been buried at the same time, it was thought that they may have died as a result of the yellow plague.

An illuminating study by Molly Miller setting the early inscribed stone monuments of the north and north-west in their historical context within the Kingdom of Gwynedd, indicated that the epidemic had a dramatic effect there. Not least with the death of Maelgwn himself whom

Gildas described as 'the island dragon . . . the first in evil' and Nennius, as the great great grandson of Cunedda who had come from the north with his eight sons 146 years previously and 'expelled the Irish with immense slaughter from those districts and they never returned again to inhabit them'.

Miller used the place-names of the eponymous cantrefs of the eight sons of Cunedda – Meirionnydd, Edeirnion, Rhufoniog, Dunoding, Aflogion, Dogfeiling, Osmaeliaun – but excluded Ceredigion, one of the three saintly lineages of Wales headed by Dewi ap Sant ap Cedig ap Ceredig. An area which in modern terms extended from Anglesey, Llŷn and old Meirionnydd northeastwards across the Conwy (the four areas where the stones are clustered) to the mouth of the Dee. In the first three the majority of the Irish and Latin inscribed stones are uniformly dated up to the period of the great plague around 550 and afterwards, as some are reused – the two at Llannor 'for an illiterate grave', or a gloss on the word priest added later on the Senacvs stone for 'the old scribal tradition required explanation'.

The earliest Ogam stone is found far to the east in Clwyd 'dedicated to Prince Similinus at Clocaenog in the 490's'. And to complicate the picture further, 'there are Irish names but no Ogams in pre-plague Anglesey' but neither are found there afterwards. In her conclusions she emphasises that such changes as may have occurred culturally especially in Eifionydd and Llŷn may not be solely or directly due to the effects of the plague.

The inscriptions in Gwynedd tend to convey more political, personal and geographic information than in other regions of Wales. At the tip of the Llŷn peninsula are the two Anelog stones at Aberdaron. Their finely cut Latin inscriptions set horizontally record the deaths of two priests On the Veracius stone this is indicated by the letters PBR as an abbreviation for presbyter and with the addition of forked serifs shows some Greek influence which dates it early, perhaps late fifth or early sixth-century. Whereas on the SENACUS stone, *PRSB/HIC/IACIT* is followed by a grammatically incorrect phrase 'with a multitude of his brethren' showing some difficulty with Latin construction and therefore carved later in the sixth-century. A second word for priest was added (perhaps much later) in a different style. This mass burial may have been due to the plague. It may also have occasioned a rare inscription to Melus the Doctor, *MELI/MEDICI* on the stone at Llangian further north, from the same period. At Llanaelhaearn the Aliortus stone tells us that he was a man of Elmet, a Brythonic kingdom in the Pennines that was overrun in the Saxon advance. Even the unusually correct form of *Hic Iacet* (here lies) among the Welsh inscriptions shows outside influence. To the east, south of Betws-y-coed, are the cluster of inscribed stones in Penmachno church recording their status as honoured Romano-British citizens and even to the period . . . 'in the time of Justinus the consul', of the eastern empire in 540. In contrast to this, Bedd Porius at Trawsfynydd states that 'he was a plain man'. Some have suggested that *PLANUS* meant leper or even Christian. A cast sits in a small caged enclosure where the original (now in the NMW, Cardiff) was found. At Gwytherin churchyard, near Llanrwst, amid a row of four small standing stones, one is inscribed to Vinnemagli. St Winifred is thought to have been a nun here although her better known well shrine and association with St Beuno who restored her severed head, is at Holywell. Finally inside Llanerfyl church is yet another unusual inscription stating that Rosteece, the thirteen year old daughter of Paterninus, lies buried here in the mound.

As well as the malignant havoc wrought on individuals in rural homesteads and small religious communities, the epidemic may have been a catalyst for the wider social upheavels of north-west Wales. In view of the date-range up to and around the mid sixth-century for many of these inscriptions, the memorials of the seventh-century are both fewer and different in form. On Anglesey, the Cadfan stone at Llangadwaladr near the court at Aberffraw is a royal memorial to one of the early kings of Gwynedd and on the mainland at Tywyn parish church, a tall thin stone slab has inscriptions running along all four sides in Welsh. It was noted first by Edward Lhwyd who made a record of it but it has since been damaged, used as a gatepost and broken near the bottom. It reads both downwards and upwards in a coarse half-uncial style that bears no comparison with the beautiful execution of that script on the Cadfan stone. The inclusion of initial crosses and the two sets of reversed brackets adds to the complexity of decipherment.

Rashly attempting to outline or put forward some coherent scenarios based on the epigraphic evidence from this period is equally unsatisfactory. Yet it does bolster in some ways the traditional historical view of the Irish and northern intrusion among the settled indigenous Romano-British population. The wider threat of the heathen English was persistent and probably evident in well-armed warrior bands and a stream of refugees.

The story of Beuno hearing English voices across the river Severn and leading his community of monks ever westward, bringing the dead back to life especially reuniting severed heads, fits the image of the saintly prince leading his people to safety. St Cadfan was another of that mold. Whether by force of arms, kin-marriage or even the influence of the new Christian church on the leading families, it is usually the victors in dynastic internecine strife who write their own history. So the Irish were displaced or inter-married with the British, as occurred in Dyfed, and the Welsh kingdom of Gwynedd emerged as the stabilising force in the region. It could invite the sons of Caw, the 'third saintly family' to move to Anglesey, perhaps to fill the vacuum left by the exudus of Irish monks. Caw was a prince of Dumnonia living in North Britain whose 'family' were forced out by the Picts and the Irish. Gildas was the most renowned saint and they were well received by Cadwallon Lawhir who granted them church lands.

However, Gabbo, whose settlement at Llangaffo continued to prosper, seems to have fallen foul of Maelgwn and was killed by some shepherds, whether as the cause or the result of the denounciations by Gildas! Cybi also of this stock came by way of Ireland and settled in the Roman fort of Caergybi or Holyhead. The church of Pabo is in the circular enclosure of Llanbabo. Pabo and Dunawd whose community came to settle on Bardsey with his son Deiniol of Bangor were related to yet another king of North Britain Coel Godebog. And finally St Elian who was a prince of the Cunedda and said to be the first of the Brythonic saints in Anglesey, had his monastery at Llanelian.

The story goes that Cadwallon offered him as much land as the saint's tame doe could run in a day. However the animal was pulled down and killed by a greyhound so Elian cursed the inhabitants and condemned them to a life of poverty. His cursing well at Old Colwyn was believed to be the most potent in Wales and was used for malign purposes until the eighteenth-century. It was Elian who founded the original settlement that became known as Penmon Priory, passing it on to his nephew Seiriol, whose own fame as a bridge and path builder was such that he even connected his second hermitage (perhaps his original monastery) on Penmaenmawr by way of a causeway over the Menai Straits. His daily perambulation across Môn (or *Anglesey* from Engles Eaye, *Island of the Angels*) to meet Cybi midway may actually refer to such a track that followed the path of the rising sun in the morning and the setting from the west, at the equinox or spring and autumn turning points of the year. What this meeting actually signified became lost in the popular lore connected with St Seiriol.

Archaeological evidence from this period such as the round church enclosures on Anglesey and the longcist burials beneath Clynnog Fawr adds to the general picture. Excavations at St Beuno's sixteenth-century church on the Llŷn peninsula revealed the foundations of a small oratory with Christian burials beneath the chapel known as Eglwys y Bedd or *Church of the Grave*. A four foot high stone has an engraved cross said to have been made by the thumb of the saint. His nearby well was famous for curing blindness and in the churchyard is a sundial carved on a tall standing stone with a flattened top. This is one of two in Wales (the other recently found at Tywyn) and is of the Anglo-Saxon type with an engraved half-circle below the hole for the gnomon representing a twelve-hour day, which was sub-divided into four parts. The more common Irish type are generally more ornate, with large D-shaped tops and subdivided by more rays.

The most startling overlap between the results of a site excavation, historical association of place and of a saintly family was at Dinas Emrys. This fort is on a ridge a few miles north-east of Beddgelert which is at the junction of two river valley systems that encircle Snowdon, to form the Aberglaslyn that eventually runs into the sea near Portmeirion. The siting of the fort on a high ridge above Llyn Dinas would have given it a strategic importance in terms of any military movement into Gwynedd. The legend of the place recounted by Nennius, concerns the building of the fort by Vortigern. Dispirited, ousted from his kingdom after the debacle of allowing the Saxons to overrun most of Britain, his druids advised him of a strong site in Gwynedd.

However, the building of the fort on the ridge was a troublesome business with the day's work and materials vanishing nightly. They then declared that what was needed was a blood sacrifice of a child without a father. When the boy was brought to the fort, he questioned them about their actions and after admitting their ignorance of the real cause of the collapsing fortress, Ambrosius or Emrys the Overlord, revealed to them that the unknown lake beneath the tower held two dragons, one red and one white who slept during the day but fought each other at night. He told them what this contest signified, red dragon of the Welsh chasing the white of the English across the lake so that the 'cloth' between them vanished. This signified the final victory would be to the Welsh and that he rather than Vortigern would build the tower, hence its name Dinas or town of Emrys.

Excavations in the mid-fifties showed that the rough stone banks were rather poorly constructed with remains of wood and stone buildings around a deeply hollowed pool inside the fort. This may correspond in part to a 'lake' under the tower, foretold by the young Ambrosius who probably claimed descent from Macsen Wledig, like Rhydderch Hael and many of the saints of the first family of Wales. It also bears close comparison to some of the divinatory rites at holy wells relying on the action of two worms or fish to foretell future events. The most surprising finds, in view of the distance inland from the sea, were shards of wine amphorae from the Eastern Mediterranean. A chi-rho symbol was found to be stamped on a piece of fine red ware pot. Clearly a high status site of the kind around the coasts of the maritime province such as Deganwy below Great Orme's Head, Dinas Powys in Glamorgan, Garranes in West Cork and Tintagel in Cornwall. It was at the monastery of the latter that the remains of Eastern ware like bowls and platters were first recognised and deemed to have been imported by the Christian aristocracy based at such large fortifications during the sixth and seventh centuries. The hillfort of Deganwy is thought to have been Maelgwn Gwynedd's powerbase. No evidence of early buildings were found but the pottery remains indicated that imported wine was drunk at the royal court, which was destroyed by the Saxons in the ninth-century according to the *Anneles Cambriae*. The dynasty was replaced by that of Merfyn Frych 'from the land of Man' whose father may have been the Guriat who is commemorated on the Manx monumental cross-slab at Maughold. Merfyn's son Rhodri who effectively became king of north and south Wales to earn the epithet 'Mawr' the Great, was killed by the English in 878.

The northern zone of the western sea province came to prominence during the Viking period before and especially after they settled in small towns. From 950 to 1100 their commerce and power politics between Dublin and Chester, an English town but with a large Viking population, turned the Irish Sea once more into an inland lake. Gruffudd ap Cynan, grandson of Cadwaladr used Vikings from Orkney to support his claim to Gwynedd in 1087. According to the *Brut y Tywysogion*, Môn was ravaged by the Black Pagans in 853. Later that century and throughout the next, unlike most of the main monastic churches that were attacked at least once (Caergybi in 961, Penmon in 971, Clynnog Fawr in 978, Tywyn in 963, Llanbadarn Fawr in 988, Llandudoch [St Dogmaels] in 907, Bangor in 1073) St David's was attacked no less than eleven times and in one of these the saint's shrine itself was stolen and stripped of its gold covering. This points up its considerable powers of recovery and the substantial resources available around the south-west.

The general picture presented by the available records is that with the exception of St David's, Wales as a whole was not a target of the Northmen unlike Ireland and Eastern England. This may have been due to the poverty of the churches in not having extensive land holdings or ecclesiastical wealth in the form of precious objects such as bells, croziers and enshrined gospel books. The hyperbole of recent discussion on this question cannot hide the fact that the seven handbells that have survived from this period are made from a poor alloy of iron and copper. The often quoted excuses for the lack of such material wealth in Wales due to internal warfare and external plunder of a small country does not hold up when applied to Ireland or even to the Isle of Man which has over one-hundred and fifty decorated cross-slabs including the Calf of Man Crucifixion carving which indicates a remarkable artistic development during this period.

References

(Summary)
Dark, K.; *Chronology of Class I inscribed stones*, in Edwards, N. and Lane, A. (Eds.); *The Early Church in Wales and the West* (Cardiff 1991).
Mathews, T.F.; *The Clash of Gods* (New Jersey, USA 1993).
Harvey, A.; *Early Literacy in Ireland C.M.C.S. 14* (Cambridge 1987).
Raftery, B.; *Drumanagh and Roman Ireland* (Archaeology Ireland, No. 35).
Maas, J.; *Letter to the Romans* (Archaeology Ireland, No. 36, Dublin 1996).

(3 Helens)
Richardson, H. & Scarry, J.; *Irish High Crosses* (Dublin 1990).
Henken, E.R.;*Traditions of the Welsh Saints* (Cambridge 1987).
Bowen, E.C.; *Saints, Seaways and Settlements* (Cardiff 1977).
Barber, C.; *More Mysterious Wales* (London 1987).
De Paor, L; *Saint Patrick's* World (Dublin 1993)
Colyer, R.; *Roads and Trackways of Wales* (Ashbourne, Derbyshire 1984).

(Roman Roads)
Lane, A. & Edwards, N.; *The Early Church in Wales & the West* (ibid).
James, H.; *Excavations at Caer, Bayvil* (Arch. Camb. 1988).
Barley, M.W. & Hanson, R.P.C.; *Christianity in Britain 300-700* (Leicester 1968).
Hughes, K.; *The Celtic Church: Is this a Valid Concept?* (C.M.C.S. No. 1, 1981).
Lane, A. & Edwards, N.; *The Early Church in Wales & the West* (ibid.)
Youngs, S.; *The Work of Angels* (British Museum Publications, 1989).
RCAHMW; *The Early Christian Period* (Glamorgan Vol. 1, Pt 3, HMSO 1976).
Doble, G.H.; *Lives of the Saints*, Ed. by D. Simon Evans (Cardiff 1971).
Davies, W.; *Wales in the Early Middle Ages* (Leicester 1982).
James, J.W.; *Chronology in the Book of Llandaff* (NLWJ No. 16, 1969/70).
Hughes, K.; *The Celtic Church: Is this a Valid Concept?* (ibid.)

(7 Watermen).
Henken, E.R.; *Traditions of the Welsh Saints* (ibid.)
Baines, E.M.; *An Unrecorded Early Christian Stone* (Arch. Camb. 1989.)
Lewis, J.M.; *A Survey of E.C.M. of Dyfed*, Welsh Antiquity (Cardiff 1976).
Sharkey, J. (Ed.); *Ogham Monuments in Wales* (Felinfach, 1992)
O'Riain, P.; *The Saints of Cardiganshire* , Cardiganshire County History 1. (Cardiff 1994).
Henken, E.R.; *Traditions of the Welsh Saints* (ibid.)
De Paor, L.; *Saint Patrick's World* (ibid.)

(Irish Sea Province)
Bowen, E.C.; *Settlements of the Celtic Saints in Wales* (Cardiff 1954).
Bowen, E.C.; *Saints, Seaways and Settlements* (ibid.)
Moore, D. (Ed.); *Irish Sea Province in Arch. & History* (Cardiff 1970).
De Paor, L.; *Saint Patrick's World* (ibid.)
Connely, D.; *The letters of St Patrick* (Maynooth, Ireland 1993).
Sharpe, R.; *Irish Saints before St Patrick*, in O'Corrain, D. etc. (Eds.) *Sages, Saints and Storytellers* (Maynooth, Ireland, 1989).

McGrail, S. *Celtic Seafaring & Transport,* in Green, M. (Ed.) *The Celtic World* (London 1995).

Thomas, C.; *Britain and Ireland in Early Christian Times* (London 1971).

Bowen, E.C.; *Britain and the British Isles,* in Moore, D., *The Irish Sea Province in Archaeology and History* (ibid.)

Cule, J. *Pistis Flava: Y Fad Felen,* in Cule, J. (Ed) *Wales and Medicine* (London 1972).

Thomas, C.; *And Shall These Mute Stones Speak?* (Cardiff 1994).

Davies, W.; *The place of healing in early Irish society,* in O'Corrain etc. (Eds) *Sages, Saints and Storytellers* (ibid.)

(Men of the North)

Alcock, E.; *Burials and Cemeteries in Scotland,* in Edwards, N. & Lane A. (Eds) *The Early Church in Wales* (ibid.)

Jarman, A.O.H.; *Aneirin – The Gododdin,* in Jarman, A.O.H. & Hughes, G.R. (Eds) *A Guide to Welsh Literature,* Vol. 1 (Cardiff 1976).

Miller, M.; *The Saints of Gwynedd* (Cardiff 1979).

Hamlin, A.; *Some Northern Sundials . . . in Rynne,* E. (Ed.) *Figures from the Past* (Dublin 1987).

Lynch, F.; *HMSO Guide to the Ancient Monuments of Gwynedd* (London 1996).

Davies, W.; *Wales in the Early Middle Ages* (ibid.)

Jones, F.; *The Holy Wells of Wales* (Cardiff 1954).

Pryce, H.; *Ecclesiastical wealth in early medieval Wales,* in Edwards, N. and Lane, A. (Eds); *The Early Church in Wales and the West* (ibid.)

Rednapp, M.; *Insular Metalwork;* in Bourke, C. (Ed.) *From the Isles of the North* (Belfast, HMSO 1995).

Rednapp, M.; *Early Christianity and its Monuments,* in Green, M. (Ed.); *The Celtic World* (ibid.)

Cubbon, A.M.; *The Art of the Manx Crosses* (Douglas 1977).

Part 2

Iconography, Design, Sculpture

The High Cross

The evolution of the Christian cross from a sign on a slab to a solid representation in stone fusing symbol and icon is akin to picking at a seamless garment for beginning and ends. In whatever shape and form on wood ceramic metal or stone, the cross represented for the followers of Christ as it had from its very inception, his crucifixion and redemption. It was a representation of the divine melding secular history into sacred image.

The few examples in Britain of the *chi-rho* monogram and its variations that gave form to the wheeled cross (often called the Celtic cross) and the linear cross were based on Greek and Latin prototypes. The monogram was formed by joining the first two letters of the name of Christ in Greek so that the X *(chi)* was cut through by the P *(rho)* and then by rotating the X into a cross shape as was done above the inscription of the Penmachno stone in Gwynedd and at St Just in Cornwall.

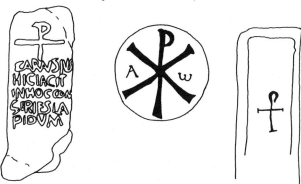

Variations of the chi-rho cross from (1-r) Penmachno, Wales; Lullingstone, Kent; St Just, Cornwall. (Drawings by M.H.)

49

A further development placed it inside a ring as in Galloway where the curve of the P still shows and finally incised as a ringed cross proper. A sixth-century example is on the Castelldwyran stone above the Latin and Ogam inscriptions to the Irish king Votipor of Dyfed designated as Protector, after the Roman style.

There is a broad date range for the changing form of the *chi-rho* monogram in Britain. One of the earliest from the fourth-century was on the mosaic floor in Dorset, now reconstructed in the British Museum, that shows a 'portrait' of Christ above the XP. In the following century after the Roman legions left, sea travel to and from the western seaboard of Britain and Ireland was probably easier and safer in the turmoil of a rapidly disintegrating empire. The small cross stamped on imported glass and wine pottery, both as a divine protection and Christian symbol, indicates the growing Christian influence among the Romano-British population.

By the middle of the sixth-century the examples above from north and south-west Wales show that the incomers from Scotland and Ireland were Christian, had formed native Celtic kingdoms but whose rulers were denounced by Gildas in his tract *De Excidio Britaniae*. The work known as *The Ruin and Conquest of Britain* survives in a tenth-century Canterbury manuscript although it had been quoted from earlier and from its style and name-forms the writer, a cleric, was well acquainted with events in Wales. This was the period of the yellow plague which probably more than any other outside event, precipitated both the veneration of the 'hundreds of saints of Ireland and Britain' who died of the fever, and the desire to seek God in lonely and out-of-the-way places.

It was this monastic impulse that also seems to have given rise to the more general use of the incised cross-slab. One tradition has it that the hermit-monk would carve his own cross to be used as an altar-stone when living and as a head-stone when dead. In the absence of other evidence, this sequence shows that almost two centuries elapsed between the earliest introduction and its use as an exotic symbol carved on stone and a further century before its countrywide spread as a holy marker of sacred ground, became commonplace. The extraordinary variety and number of (Group 2) incised stones from all parts of Wales based on the Latin type or with an incorporated ring-cross is from the later seventh-century period when the tradition of local carving was clearly established.

It is possible that the transitional types of cross and cross-slabs with limited Celtic decoration were in use together. This continued even when the free-standing high crosses were being carved. For instance in the church of Llandyfaelog fach, three miles north of Brecon is a tall narrow stone slab with a central figure wearing a long tunic with a spear and dagger. Briamail/Flou is inscribed beneath. Celtic decoration surrounds him and the cross above his head. It is a double band Latin type with stafford knots on the arms and shaft creating a continuous 'cross of eternity'.

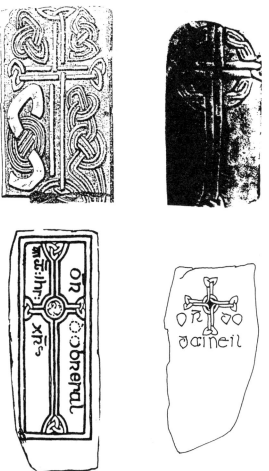

Inscribed cross-slabs from Wales (1-r) at Llandyfaelog fach and Llangyfelach; from Ireland at Glendalough and Clonmacnois. (Drawings by M.H.)

A broken slab, now reset into the interior wall of the nave of Llangyfelach church has a similar type cross set in false relief but with a decorative ring placed inside the terminals and CRUX XPI inscribed alongside which has been dated to the ninth-century. A pillar stone of the same period, in the porch of Llanwnnws church in Ceredigion shows yet another example of the double ring band type with stafford knots at the terminals but with four round bosses set inside the ring and the arms of the cross. It too has an inscription in Latin set in twelve lines.

In Reefert church at Glendalough in Ireland, a 1.4m high slab has same endless band form of cross with a ring around the centre of the arms, set inside a rectangular frame. At Clonmacnois the cross is in the Greek equal-armed form with 'or do daneil', pray for Daniel, inscribed around and beneath it. On Iona is yet another example from the same ninth/tenth-century period but with a square interlaced circle in the centre.

Hundreds of such inscribed slabs with partial or complete decoration from the monasteries of Ireland have been recorded by Macalister. In contrast, fourteen grave-slabs with or without inscriptions (RCAMW Class C types) have been listed in the Vale of Glamorgan. This is from the region with the highest and most representative number of Early Christian monuments in Wales. It is fairly obvious that comparisons with most cross types here can be found in Ireland except for the wheeled stumpy slab-cross in South Wales and the free-standing high crosses with Anglian crossheads. Both illustrate the extreme localisation of cross carving and the often crucial differences of form between Welsh, Irish, Pictish and English high crosses.

However there are sufficient examples in Wales to illustrate what F. Henry called the emergence of the cross from the one dimensional slab into the relief or shaped three-dimensional threshold of the 'free' cross. The cross of Houelt is free-standing with a large circular 'disc' head. The squared ends of the equal-armed cross are decorated with diagonal key-patterns that emphasise the suggestion of a ringed cross potent in relief, reminiscent of Pictish Christian art.

The cross that exemplified this transition for the renowned Irish scholar was the 2.5m high St Patrick's cross on the roadside by Carndonagh church in Co. Donegal. The red sandstone shaped cross, flanked by two small decorated pillars, is carved in shallow relief with broad bands of interlace throughout. The front shaft has a figure of Christ

Cross of Houelt, Llanilltud Fawr, Vale of Glamorgan.

in a long tunic with arms outstretched. Henry places this cross in the seventh-century because of the similar decoration in the Book of Durrow, however other scholars date it to the ninth and even the tenth-century.

In the nearby graveyard is a 1.6m high pillar-cross decorated on all four sides. The W face shows a flabellum with a cross on the fan made up of seven decorated triangular segments, flanked by two figures above a marigold cross. The E face shows a crucifixion above two figures and an equal-armed decorated cross. This side of the densely packed iconic stone bears a curious resemblance to a cross-slab in Meifod church in Powys. It too has a crucifixion in a small wheel cross placed above a larger highly decorated cross set in slight relief and surrounded by a myriad of small decorative motifs.

It seems almost as if it was carved from memory or description of the Carndonagh crosses. There is another curious interplay of influences with the stone crosses that are around the ruined St Dogmael's Abbey above the Teifi estuary. Some of them show the same liturgical fan as well as the Maltese type or marigold pattern cross. There is a small figure of Christ in a long garment with outstretched arms beneath the cross formy on the large stone from here that is now in National Museum of Wales.

Not far away at Llanychaer in the Gwaun valley is a 1.2m high pillar stone with the same combination of ritual objects and wheeled crosses incised on all four sides. There is also an image of the crucified Christ with wide fingers splayed. The combination of icon and image on each face but showing a new variation or slightly different motif makes it almost a prototypical free-standing cross. Perhaps one of the few precursors of the truly decorated high cross in Wales.

Rubbing (half-size) of detail from stone pillar in Llanychaer churchyard, Pembrokeshire.

54

The crudeness of the figuration is a noticeable feature on some other stone fragments. At Llanhamlach in Powys, two figures stand beneath a cross of splayed ends, with arms outstretched in that ancient attitude of prayer, and surrounded by rough interlacing and fret symbolic designs. Because of the breasts? on one, they are said to represent Mary with St John on the left. Another version of this popular scene is carved on a tall slab from Nash Manor in the Vale of Glamorgan. However closer examination reveals they are likely to be the lance and sponge bearers that are traditional adjuncts in Irish and Northern stone carving of the crucifixion. The figure on the left is holding a square (sponge?) and the other has what appears to be the end of a pole protruding downward between the legs.

The large disc cross at Llangan is now weathered but it shows Christ in a short tunic with Stephaton and Longinus crouching below the outstretched arms and open palms. The literal tendency and crudeness of the *Orans* type figuration on these and on the cross-shaft at Llanfrynach, near Brecon, may appear almost primitive. Especially in comparison with the well-finished carving on the large Celtic crosses and cross-slabs. However, both are parallel decorative conventions, even using the same motifs. What we might now term high and low art.

Cross-slab from Llanhamlach, Powys. *Cross-slab from Llanfrynach, Powys.*

However, the primitive work can and often does mask the depths of symbolic meaning the carvers aspired towards. Likewise as it is clear from some of the Celtic crosses, the attention to detail in abstract designs often verges on a vacousness that is only rescued by the delicate form of the actual crosshead. The Carew cross is a case in point. The Cadw guidebook describes it as magnificent which on a monumental level it is, but spiritually? The poor comparisons made between it and English or Irish high crosses due to its clumsiness and lack of proportion are in many ways justified, yet the facility of the mason in setting out its large abstract panels is very evident. The skilfulness of medieval carvers is undeniable even from the smallest of stone fragments that have survived in Wales. From the point of view of the current revival of Celtic design and its application to jewellery, iconic imitations and other tourist kitch, the question of function is subsumed under another, i.e. what does it mean? And eventhough as we have seen the carving on stone of the Christian cross was subject to a series of stylistic revivals with shifts in type, size and material, it functioned as a holy religious object. In its later monumental phase the memorial cross was probably considered more a secular symbol than a sacred object.

The square-armed ring cross carved on the pillar in Tregaron churchyard, Ceredigion, is generally considered as transitional from the incised cross slab to the more sculptured cross in relief. The faint prong extending from the ring of the cross brings to mind a number of (Group 2) crosses with pointed ends of a late date that are located from Anglesey southwards.

In Llanarth church is an inscribed but undecorated Latin cross set out clearly against the slab. And further up the Ceredigion coast at Llanbadarn Fawr is the massive form of what is considered to be a shaped cross. It was buried up to its arms in the graveyard near the reclining high cross. When unearthed it was found to be somewhat pointed and set in a small tombstone dated 1755. It is now inside the church next to the tall decorated cross. This block of sandstone is 1.4m high with a deeply incised edge moulding around the cruciform 'head'. Below it, in the middle of a curved incised panel is a round hole. It does suggest a belly-button on a fat mother-figure. Perhaps it originally represented a goddess that was reshaped and chiselled into the more acceptable form of a cross. There are also what is considered to be traces of carving on the head but this in fact may be due to defacing.

Stone pillar cross, Llanbadarn Fawr, Ceredigion. (Drawing by M.H.)

W.G. Thomas in a new County History even sees the curious raised carving at the back of the figure as 'something like a Greek omega' whereas the account of the uplifting of the stone makes no bones about it being of phallic origin.

One could conceivably view these three examples in terms of typology as a form of evolution from the slab to a solid shaped cross, especially as they all are in the same area of west Wales.

A more significant reminder of the transition of the shaped cross emerging from the stone can be seen from two crosses in mid Wales. In fact they could almost be a mirror-image of the tall ringed cross receding into, or standing out from, the slab. In Llanrhaeadr-ym-Mochnant the 1.7m high stone is decorated with interlace and fretwork leaving the cross itself bare with an inscription running along the central arm of the ringed head. On the stone inside the church at Llowes, the surrounding area has been chipped off leaving the large ringed-cross to stand out in stark relief.

The shaft and arms are decorated with seven large 'open' diamond-shape patterns that add an architectural touch to the 2.1m high x 0.9 wide x 0.26 deep rectangular slab. Both the decoration and the ring-cross are clearly influenced by Irish free-standing crosses. The direct antecedents

St Meilog's Cross, Llowes, Powys.
(Drawing by M.H.)

Inscribed pillar cross, Llanrhaeadr-ym-Mochnant, Powys. (Drawing by M.H.)

or models upon which the earliest high crosses were based are scholarly questions that have wider implications for the history of early Christianity on these islands.

Some scholars favour an insular process in terms of the long tradition of stone working as the crucible in which a foreign influence or object can create a whole new style. The vital spark being the necessary power and wealth of a particular influential group on the socio-religious feeling of the time. The absorption of outside styles into the local mainstream is in fact one of the vital hallmarks of Celtic art from its earliest beginnings in the Hallstat period to late medieval art. Even the constant borrowing from one medium to another was an essential part of the creative act.

A different view of the evolved growth of the high cross, sets it in the wider context of Christianity. Part of the continuous influx from Rome as the centre of the church to the Celtic periphery. From visits to the Holy Land and even further afield in the Byzantine world where cross-slabs on plinths, crosses on pillars and free-standing monuments with biblical scenes were common from the sixth-century. The extent of such iconic influences and plagerisms of Roman liturgy on the great Irish crosses are still subject to debate in journals, symposia and in an increasing number of new publications.

It is notoriously difficult to date stone crosses with any degree of certainty. Francoise Henry based her mid-eighth-century axis for the first flowering of the high crosses of Western Ossory (an area in north Munster) on the shift of manuscript styles from Northumbria to Iona to Ireland. On the transference of one medium to another. From the pen of the scribe to the fine tool of the metalworker to the iron chisel of the stonemason. From each there was a natural decay of subtlety and yet the highest art forms in all media are almost totally self-referential.

West face of South Cross, Ahenny, Co. Tipperary.

The often repeated explanation for the large bosses on the ringed crossheads as stylistic borrowings (from the use of unadorned round 'cups' to hide the joins on the metal crosses) suggests some now lost models for these earliest ring-crosses that some scholars now date to a later period than Henry. The two Ahenny crosses have five bosses on each face and two others of the Ossory group have five on the west side but only one on the east face. The extruding bosses, create a delicate visual balance between the receding ring and heavily moulded decorated cross. They help the eye to play on the ring of the true Celtic cross set within the more monumental aspect of base, shaft, ringhead, and beehive top-hat that the symbolic form of the high cross dictated.

The differing viewpoints of the historians can be summed-up as based on the art and iconography of the outer form and its intrinsic meaning in terms of Christianity and religious liturgy. Of course, both approaches often overlap to show how one might more meaningfully view the high cross in its broader context.

It is also possible that the earliest free-standing cross in each region was created by a carver's creative skill. In the manner that great artists can almost pull together a range of common ideas 'that are in the air' and seemingly create an entirely new form. Once in place in its monastic setting, the landscape accommodates the newest form of religious monument. It quickly re-arranges itself so that what at first may have seemed like an exotic import becomes part of the outer order of the religious life. And in the large monasteries of Ireland such a high cross would have naturally inspired other, perhaps less well endowed, houses to commission slightly less sophisticated crosses. It is important to remember in any discussion of Irish high crosses that roughly half of the estimated two-hundred and fifty that have survived are of the plain and undecorated kind. That such a high proportion of seemingly undifferiented free-standing crosses are thought to be unworthy of consideration by many scholarly commentators may be in part due to the overwhelming presence of the massive open-ring type that is especially Irish and popularly associated with 'the land of saints and scholars'. But undue emphasis on the evolution of the highly wrought cross tends to obscure the importance of parallel carving traditions.

There is one mention of a cross being set-up in a monastic enclosure in Wales, in a charter from Llancarfan appended to Lifris' *Life of St Cadog*. A factor in common with both Anglo-Saxon and Welsh high crosses is that their presence tends to indicate early ecclesiastical sites that have been lost in subsequent church rebuilding. In the aftermath of the mid-seventh-century Synod of Whitby the stone masons, mentioned by Bede, as introduced to build the continental style churches in England may also have been instrumental in popularising stone sculpture. For craftsmen already highly skilled in carving wood, such a step is easy when the demand and the religious fervour of the period is taken into account.

The Northumbrians later helped introduce Christian forms and themes into an already highly evolved Pictish art of stone carving. Again according to Bede, King Nechton's request in 710 for guidance and workers to bring the church and his kingdom closer to Rome may have been at the expense of the much older Columban mission of Iona but yet it played a part in creating the vibrant Celtic art of this period.

Later still in the complex melting pot of variation, style and influences the wheel-headed cross was introduced into western Britain in the first half of the tenth-century by Viking colonials from Ireland. And not before the end of that century did their carving in relief reach Scandinavia. It is the amalgamation of Norse-Celtic ornament and Anglo-Scandinavian wheelhead that is the distinctive feature of the free-standing high crosses in Wales.

The Free-standing Monuments

Complete high crosses, free-standing or on pedestals, can be counted on the fingers of both hands. Their geographical distribution makes a rough circuit of the country. They can be sub-divided, almost regionally, into type or with similar features such as Anglian crossheads or disc-eared as on the Penmon crosses. The Padarn cross near Aberystwyth was carved from a single block of stone. Although the original shaft of St Brynach's at Nevern was even longer if one adds the unadorned eight feet below ground level, its head is separate and carved from a softer stone.

Similar to the Nevern in respect of the different materials used for both shaft and cross, the Carew cross is a composite of parts. Also in the south-west, the smaller Penally cross was carved from a single slab but with markedly Scandinavian decoration on its shaft. It has a similar Anglian crosshead characterised by wide curving arms of an equal armed cross lying on the outer ring, as both the Nevern churchyard cross and the one in the corner of the grounds of Carew Castle.

In south Wales, the Coychurch cross was re-erected after a fall of masonary from the church tower in the late nineteenth-century broke it into three pieces. It now stands in the corner of St Crallo's Church. The Llandough pillar cross has a short shaft above the ornate collar and is without its crosshead. However the sketch by Lhwyd in 1690 shows what looks like the remains of a ringed head on a shaft not much taller than the present one. The shaft in Llandaff Cathedral in Cardiff seems to be similar in shape and size so perhaps its original crosshead and pedestal may have been of the same type as the Llandough at Penarth.

The cross of Confelyn which once stood in the village street outside the courtyard of Margam Abbey, is disc-headed and a composite cross. The Houelt cross is a free-standing slab in St Illtud's (west) Church in Llanilltud Fawr. These two are the most elaborate and complete of a large number of smaller, broken and fragmented crosses from the Vale of Glamorgan.

There are a few large sculptured crosses in mid Wales with distinct styles of form and decoration such as the Neuadd Siarman pillar cross in the Brecon Museum, the slab-cross of St Meilig inside Llowes church and the tall Latin wheel-cross in the church of Llanrhaeadr-ym-Mochnant.

Excluding some of the south Wales crosses which will be considered in detail later is it possible to consider the above monuments as a particular group with certain defined characteristics? Or is the type, size and dimensions of their parts so disperate that it is better to view them as individual local examples of medieval art. Especially as they are now so few in number. However such considerations have not been generally applied to all the Welsh high crosses so it may be a useful way of opening up a discussion. It is the iconography, the style and use of certain motifs on the shaft panels and crosshead that is usually regarded as the defining characteristics of the Celtic cross. One can refine this surface perception further by size of the actual panels, the manner in which the designs have been carved, by the stone chipped away from the slab to help outline the overall shape of the cross, or the way areas have been left in relief to highlight the internal decorative elements. The last is especially common with the making of the wheelhead or the cross within the cross. There is also the fusion with northern stylistic elements on the Penally and the Penmon crosses.

These factors may be conditional on the material used, sandstone or the harder granites, and on the limitation of choice that probably was the most overriding factor in terms of the shape and combination of design motifs. We know next-to-nothing about the masons or those who directly commissioned the crosses.

An Irish master builder named Illwri (O'Leary?) is mentioned in the *Life of Cadog*, as coming to Llancarfan in a wagon with his family, looking for work. There are the names in some of the inscriptions such as: 'Conmarch painted (in stone) this text at the command of his king' on the Pillar of Eliseg or 'Conbelyn put up this cross for the soul of (his father) Rhys' or 'Moridic raised this stone' on a decorated cross-slab from Powys.

The cross at Whitford may still be in situ, isolated in an open space and protected by an iron railing. But with the possible exception of the Nevern cross, still standing in the churchyard position where it was placed sometime around 1000 AD and the Llandough pillar-cross of the same period, the other crosses are now either inside churches or museums.

It means that the former appreciation of a high cross amid the cluster of later gravestones set against the background of the church is lost. It also means that the spiritual rationale for the placing of such large stone crosses in the south side of the churchyard, standing upon sacred ground of an even more ancient clas or early ecclesiastical settlement, is yet another forgotten reality of the past.

One can see in the general Welsh preference for the term Celtic (that originally defined the style of ornament) as a way of incorporating an old Catholic heritage without bruising present-day religious sensibilities. Here 'Celtic' is now commonly used to prefix the early saints, their church and the medieval decorated crosses. So it is used in this book as with terms to describe crosses such as free-standing, cross-slab or pillar – and their crossheads as being 'eared' disced or wheel-shaped. The conventional usage of the Celtic high crosses is followed for those erect stone monuments that are sculpted and decorated with our traditional ethnic designs. Part of the developed repertoire of Celtic Christian art that has its roots in the European La Tene and the earlier Hallstat phase of stone and metalwork.

The implication of stature, physical presence as a stone cross made to be seen, in the term 'high cross' is bourne out in the diagram showing the relative heights of each. They are of two main categories. Those standing from 3m (9 feet) upwards with the tallest slightly above 4m (13 feet) and those around the 2m (6.6 feet) in height. The Carew cross can be clearly seen to be one of the tallest as well as bulky. And from the tall group, the Llanbadarn Fawr cross is one of the narrowest. In fact it is almost 11 inches square on all sides.

Of the twelve crosses, four have bases if the Dyserth cross with the similarly decorated pedestal found in the church wall, and the Llandough

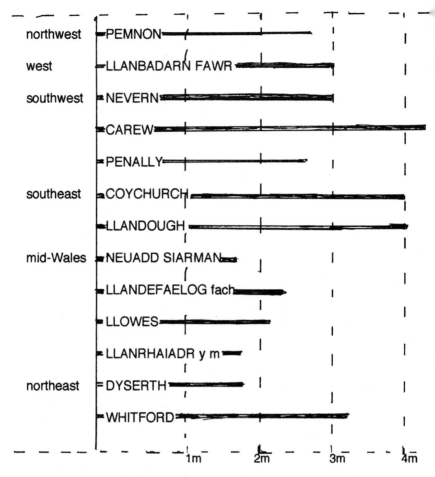

Diagram with relative heights of Welsh freestanding crosses.

which is at present without its crosshead (sketched in 1694) are included. Eight are free-standing and with the exception of the Nevern and Llanbadarn Fawr crosses where the ratio of width to breath indicates a more monumental aspect, the rest are usually described as cross-slabs.

They are also shown in terms of location. With the exception of the Penally cross the tall crosses are from the south-west group, from both corners of the north and from one area in the south-east. The smaller crosses are from mid Wales. This confirms much of what has been set out in the introductory remarks above. However it may confirm the location of schools or workshops where the crosses were crafted and the direction or thrust of influences from elsewhere that are an acknowledged part of the Welshness of these high crosses. Irish and Northumbrian influences in the west and south-east; Northern in Anglesey and English along the border areas of mid Wales.

Most of the large crosses are dated in a time-band of a few hundred years from the end of the ninth-century to the late eleventh-century. In many ways it seems to have been an ebullient, though little known period of the Welsh Church prior to the onslaught of the reforming Norman clerics. The political kingdoms that had once claimed noble ancestry from the Roman period, were now well established. Leaders such as Rhodri Fawr (the Great) who died in 878; his grandson Hywel Dda I (the Good) founder of Deheubarth who issued his own coinage and is credited with a code of law; and Gruffudd ap Llywelyn who died just before the Normans landed at Hastings effectively ruled large areas of Wales.

Individual rulers were often at loggerheads but they did endow many churches as can be deduced from the burials and royal inscribed stones in Gwynedd, Powys and in the south-east. The four established ecclesiastical foundations with associated bishops at Bangor, St David's, Llandeilo and Llandaff were vying for supremacy. However, the often quoted remark by Giraldus on the lax morals of the Welsh clergy, and that the church of Llanbadarn Fawr like many others in Wales and Ireland had a degenerate lay abbot rather than a Roman bishop as its head, obscures his attempt to elevate St David's above the rest and on a par with Canterbury.

He quotes Bede's story of the seven British bishops of Wales who turned on their heels and walked out of the meeting because Augustine refused to rise in their presence and that they were now only four in his time, towards the close of the twelfth-century. The seven bishops were of Hereford, Worcester, Llandaff, Bangor, St Asaph, Llanbadarn Fawr and Glamorgan. At least some of these locations can be recognised in the list of complete high crosses. The omission of St David's at this period might well answer the puzzlement that some writers have expressed about the lack of a Celtic high cross in the patron see of Wales.

We know something of the association of one ecclesiastical family with Llanbadarn Fawr, of the intellectual and spiritual influence of Sulien. He studied in Scotland and then in Ireland for ten years prior to his return to Ceredigion as 'a man distinguished in learning'. He served as Bishop of St David's in the 1070's and later in the 1080's after Bishop Abraham was killed in a Viking raid. Being educated by such a father, the work of two of his four sons, show marked Irish influences. Rhygyfarch wrote the *Life of David* which makes use of the Irish saints Lives. The Psaltar, now in Trinity College Dublin, was decorated by his brother.

The illuminated parts of the text are formed by what has been termed 'knotted-wire' initials coloured in red, yellow and green inks and surrounded by orange-red dots. Ieuan also decorated three carpet pages and used a variety of motifs such as animal-heads, spiral fishtail and foliate terminals to indicate breaks in the text of the Martyrology of Rhygyfarch from the same manuscript. Written at Llanbadarn Fawr between 1064 and 1082 during the time when the De Trinitate of St Augustine was also illuminated by Ieuan. These are the only extant examples of complete manuscripts executed in Wales, although Nancy Edwards in examining the nature of the Irish connection suggests that Llanbadarn Fawr may have drawn upon a lost native tradition of manuscript illumination.

The concise dating of these manuscripts is unusual when compared with that of Irish and Northumbrian MS but it may point to the possible carving of the Padarn high cross at this period or even earlier. E.G. Bowen who lived and taught at Aberystwyth for many years has written extensively on the settlements of the Celtic saints. Padarn's parents are believed to have come from Brittany to Wales and the saint himself was trained for the religious life in Ireland. A comparison with the teaching and lithurgy Padarn might have received with that of Sulien hundreds of years later could be instructive in relation to Irish and Welsh monasticism. However as was common with many Celtic saints returning to their birthplace he set up monastic communities on route in Wales and in the Devon/Cornwall area. The original llan or holy enclosure, named after the saint, in time became the clas (a Welsh word that denotes a centre, perhaps even a mother church, of early monastic activity) of Llanbadarn Fawr. Pre-eminent in the west long before Sulien's time when it was absorbed into the episcopal see of St David's. Later when it became a Benedictine house, a cell of Gloucester, its secular school continued.

Contrary to the usual much later dating of the high cross that once stood in the churchyard, Bowen thought it was carved in the middle of the eighth-century. If correct would make it one of the earliest of the decorated high crosses. Its biblical scenes on the front and zoomorphic panel on the reverse side are rare exceptions to the overtly abstract

Detail of high cross at Llanbadarn Fawr, Ceredigion.

designs that distinguish Welsh crosses as a separate group from Irish, Anglo-Saxon and Pictish monuments.

The three scenes on the front of the cross are a pair of back-to-back animals, the seated figure of Christ with ringleted hair and a spiral of folding drapery and below it a panel that may show Jacob wrestling with the Angel. The figure could equally represent Padarn holding a crozier of Continental type. On the twelfth-century Doorty cross at Kilfinora, Co. Clare, is a full figure in relief representing Christ as Abbot of the World with a spiral crozier in the same position and beneath him are two ecclesiastics trusting their Irish tau and round-headed croziers into a beast below. As with the panel on the front of the Penmon cross, showing the Temptation of St Anthony, all such scenes are common on Irish crosses.

St Brynach's high cross has been described by Romilly Allen as the most perfect example of its kind now remaining in Wales. Allen was the editor of the influential journal Archaeologia Cambrensis for many years and his subdivision of the Early Christian monuments of Scotland into four classes led Nash-Williams to a similar schema for the Welsh monuments. His Group 1 and 2 included the inscribed stones and cross decorated slabs from the sixth to the ninth centuries. Group 3 comprised the medieval decorated stone crosses and Group 4 the later Romanesque sculpture.

Although why this latter group should have been included under Early Christian monuments seems a case of cramming in as much Welsh decorative art as possible. Even more problematical is his lumping of all the Ogam inscribed stones together as Class 1 when only some of them have carved Christian crosses.

In north Pembrokeshire where many of the Ogam inscribed stones are located, archaeological excavations have revealed pagan and Christian burials together in the same ground. At Caer, Bayvil, the Christians were interred in rows of simple 'dug' graves on an east/west axis as late as the middle of the seventh-century alongside full cist burials dug into the round bank. More recently at Eglwyswrw church single burials facing east/west have been discovered alongside small stone cist burials at the edge of the present graveyard. The assumptions behind the Nash-Williams criteria of all Ogam stones being Christian memorials would now seem questionable.

Romilly Allen set out some principles underlying the decorative art of the Celtic crosses. Much of what he termed the leading characteristics have been applied in the carving of the Nevern cross. The prominence given to the framed panels and that each panel is complete with a finished design. The use of diagonal setting-out lines within rectangular panels using interlace, fret and other patterns. Carving out the different panels in combination of these with almost geometrical perfection. And finally the superiority of the abstract designs over any figurative work. In his description of the evolution of interlacing from regular plaits into the various kinds and manner of knotwork, he maintained the best place to study it was on the Welsh crosses. He explained with clear diagrams each stage of the eight different kinds of knot. From the shape of the regular Greek fret pattern, he showed the variety of the Celtic forms achieved by the use of diagonal key patterns in the high crosses under review.

The aesthetic distinctions we might make between carving styles such as Celtic or Northumbrian does not appear to have been an important issue for those who commissioned the monumental crosses of Wales. Equally the question of transition between the highly decorated exterior and the lesser carving that was deemed necessary in the completion of a stone cross would not be important then. Each cross when erected in the open was a holy object to be venerated as such, no matter how crude or unfinished the decoration might seem in the pursuit of the ideal Celtic cross. Unlike some later Irish religious art historians, Allen looked at the total number of decorated crosses and cross fragments available for the study of Celtic Christian art in Wales. Metalwork is limited and manuscripts few. What remains are ornamented slabs and erect monuments in the shape of a cross. He showed the development of Celtic sculpture here by extrapolating the different formal ways the carvers applied their range of patterns.

Once the principle of how to change these basic shapes had been grasped, it would seem that there should not be any limit to either the amount or variety of motifs used. However this was clearly not the case with those who carved the crosses. Other factors must have been operative at the time to limit their degree of choice. There was also the limitations in terms of the hard stone used and the necessary jigging about with the forms of the knot and interlacing to fit in with the overall concept of the work as well as the size and shape of the panels from which the motifs would be carved. The Llanbadarn Fawr cross was carved from a single module of stone, thought to have come from the Llŷn peninsula. All four sides and the head were minutely decorated. Measuring the shaft to built a wooden prototype revealed that although all four sides were roughly the same eleven inches width along the entire length, the actual corners of the shaft were 'out of true'.

The indications being that each surface of the shaped stone was carved horizontally with the result that there is a curious twist to it which is not noticeable to the eye when upright. The corded edges of the cross may have helped this perception. Perhaps the carver worked-up from the original relic which in life of the saint is said to have been given to him as a gift by the Patriarch of Jerusalem. The Bysantine image carved on the front representing both Christ in Majesty and Padarn as Abbot of the Mother Church would certainly not have been on the relic that Ieuan ap Sulien exaults in an *englyn* written in the margin of a manuscript.

'Much accomplishing,
Much loved it gives protection
Its holy power reaching the limits of the three continents.
No other relic can be compared with Cyrwen –
A wonderful gift – Padarn's staff.'

Nevern cross, Pembrokeshire.

The Nevern high cross presented a different set of problems to the maker. The roughly squared shaft of Preseli dolerite (the same rock formation from which some of the Stonehenge bluestones originated) was probably set-up before much of the carving was completed. The overall panels and designs roughed out by the master mason for the apprentices to do most of the chipping and shaping. Three of the six panels with the T-fret motifs were geometrically laid out in rations of 2:1 on the N face and the two on the W face were in ratio of 3:2. In contrast to this the nine large panels with knotwork and interlace have no such mean ratios with the designs within the panels done almost freehand. The tops of the S and N faces were chamfered in order to make a decent fit into the crosshead with the result that the knotwork patterns followed the shaping of the shaft. The top two designs have an almost plastic quality with their more

70

rounded prototypes further down the shaft. It would appear then that the crosshead, as on the Carew cross, was commissioned from elsewhere and when it arrived adjustments were made to the design of the shaft.

The mason on the spot attempted an elegant solution in order to have the cross as attractive to the eye as possible. The juxtaposition of the panels around the dns inscription on the main W face shows how the six geometrical panels were also subtlely altered. The left-hand side of the bottom panel was two inches longer than the thirty inches on the right. The finished ratios of those on the right upward are 10:9, 10:9, 10:9½ while those on the left are 10:9, 11:8.5, 11:8.5. In comparison the ratios on its companion panel at the bottom of the N face shows that the height and width of the eight panels expand evenly upward as 6:7, 7:7, 7.5:7, 8:7.5.

Rubbing (quarter-size) of fret-design from S. face of Nevern cross. (Photograph by M.H.)

Rubbing (half-size) of fret-design from Carew cross, Pembrokeshire. (Photograph by M.H.)

The patterns on some of the small slabs found north of the river Teifi in Ceredigion are similar to those on the Nevern cross. It may be that they were in the nature of trial pieces, perhaps even the dispersed discards of a workshop's stock-in-trade. The cross-heads in Llandeilo church are yet another indication that a different style from the Anglian type were also being carved in this area. A style suggestive of the cross on the carpet page of the *Book of Chad*. The manuscript was placed on the altar of Llandeilo Fawr as a gift. A note in the margin says the saint was asked to witness it.

In his detailing of carved patterns on Irish crosses, H.S. Crawford suggests that in spite of their variety the ancient carvers adhered to specific types. And the other main observation was their limited use of motifs with the spiral, fret, star and knot. The artists who carved the decoration on the high crosses preferred, or were expected, to confine themselves to certain well-established conventions but were free to modify the arrangement and proportions as they choose. This has enabled the designs to be classified into distinct classes of ornament such as decorative (abstract), symbolic (biomorphic) and pictorial (living forms). He adds a rider that it is often difficult to ascertain a specific meaning from the use of abstract designs, merely to please the eye and/or fill-up space on a stone and that pictorial motifs do sometimes have symbolic intent.

On the hundreds of Irish carved crosses, the most common types of abstract ornament are the interlace and fret patterns; the spiral and star forms set into rectangular, circular and semi-circular shapes, and as border infills. The earliest eight-century group such as the exquisitely carved Ahenny ringed high crosses from Co. Tipperary contain all the above classes of ornament as well as the stepped base, large bosses and the 'beehive' shaped cap on top. The heavy moulding of the arms, ring and shaft tends to counterpoint the interlaced and spiral decoration.

In a sense the Irish ringed high cross as a composite work of art is complete from the earliest phase. In the century or two that elapsed between this first flowering of Irish decorative stonework and the carving of the Welsh free-standing cross with its Northern influenced crosshead and distinctive set combinations of panels decorated in fret and knotwork patterns, a common repertoire of Celtic decoration appears to have been well established. In relation to the other classes of Irish ornament listed above, zoomorphic designs make an occasional appearance here. Panels on the Penally and Llanbadarn Fawr crosses show pairs of 'affronting beasts' and interlace terminating in beasts' heads. Pictorial designs such as the Temptation of St Anthony in the Desert on the Penmon Cross, can be seen on the Kells market cross and on the Moone and Castledermot crosses in Co. Kildare, and the group of horse-riders carved on a few pedestals here, are also included on the above as well as the affronted animal motifs. Animals in combat, whether in the form of horses, dogs, lions, birds and 'beasts' appear to have been equally popular on Northern as well as Pictish crosses.

Side panels of Whitford cross, Flintshire.

The Maes Achwyfan cross in north-east Wales shows considerable Northern influence in the use of large areas of decorative carving as well as its iconography. Carved from a single monolith the cross is the tallest of its type here. The triquetra knots that form the curved cross around an embellished boss is similar to crosses in Chester. There was a large Viking enclave here during the tenth-century with an established tradition of monumental carving. The decoration on the shaft is related to Northumbrian carving in low relief with large panels of plait, diagonal cross patterning and spiral loops around an animal-headed demon. The figure on the side panel with a raised arm and axe between its legs suggests a fertility-god or hero-god. The combination of Christian and heathen iconography is not uncommon on the English crosses of northern Britain.

First recorded by Edward Lhwyd and published in Gibson's 1695 edition of Camden's *Britannia*, the Whitford cross has been the subject of more discussion by antiquarians than any other Welsh cross. Thomas Pennant was born near here and in his 1781 Tour in Wales, recounted the local name for it, Maen Achwyfan or *'the Stone of Lamentations'* by which it has been known ever since. It is probably on the spot where originally erected, a mile or so west of the village which is situated not far off the main road to Holywell. Itself the locus of one of the most famous pilgrimage shrines of medieval Wales.

The Cross within the Cross

The large decorated cross is actually composed of two crosses. The stone edifice itself which can be in the form of a free-standing slab or a composite structure set up on a large stone base and the cross-head on top of a shaft. They were carved in various forms that have been given descriptive names or types. In Wales the most distinctive sculpted forms are the 'Anglian' type in the south-west, the disc-head and wheelhead in the south coastal region, and a sub-species called the 'eared' disc-head found along the north coast. Another group of crosses in mid Wales have the 'hammer' crosshead scooped or scalloped out of the top of the shaft.

The Penmon 'eared' disc-heads are in the shape of a disc in the form of a Celtic cross with protrusions or 'ears' beyond the ring at the top, left and right arms. The head on the main cross has fractured and the smaller one illustrates 'the cross within the cross' being carved from a single stone.

Wheelheads (1-r) of Brecon, Llanbadarn Fawr, Whitford and the Penmon cross which lost an 'ear' when reused as a lintel.

The Whitford cross has a small disc-head set on a tapering shaft nearly 3m tall. The cross head is formed of small equal-arms splaying outward from a huge central boss and surrounded by a double ring. The east face has four triquetra knots set in the arms of the cross. The knots on the west face have been compressed around the ringed boss, marked in a series of criss-cross lines that in fact form yet another cross shape. A cable ring runs around the larger cross, offsetting the head against the three large panels on the shaft below.

The Llanbadarn Fawr cross has the head scooped out of the top of the monolith. Front and back has a key-pattern and irregular knotwork around a small central ring and boss. The front also has a tiny cross set between the head and the decorated panels of the shaft.

The Neuadd Siarman pillar-cross is another of this type but with the ring showing behind the rounded interspaces. The central rose of interlace is surrounded by fine interlaced patterns forming the crosshead which is defined by heavy moulding. The moulding and the interlace continues the length of the 1.7m shaft.

The Nevern cross has a separate crosshead of the 'Anglian' type with four curving arms joined by a double ring and with four small ringed pellets in the interspaces. Decorating the four arms is a corded set of interlacing surrounding a small boss on the west face. The neck has three panels, the centre one carved with a double knot on both sides. The crosshead sits ungainly on the shaft.

Wheelheads (1-r) of Nevern, Penally and Carew crosses.
(Drawings by M.H.)

The Carew cross is of the same type but has a ring where the hollows between the arms show through. It also has a slightly larger shouldered neck which also sits uneasily on the shaft. The curved arms on the front of the crosshead have weathered leaving only a slight suggestion of interlace on the bottom one. The neck has a large panel of T-fret above three smaller panels of key-fret patterns. The back has a three-line linear cross with curved ends that mirror the overall shape of the ringed cross. Below it the neck has a similar arrangement of panels as on the front but filled with triangular patterns.

The Penally crosshead is similar to the two above, with splaying moulded arms set out in relief from the surrounding ring. The interlace on the front and back of each arm is slightly more intricate than on the Nevern Cross. The central 'rose' on both faces is composed of a four-sided loop. The back and front of the highly decorated shaft begins immediately below the bottom of the crosshead. Carved from a single stone, the end of the shaft was left undecorated as a kind of false base.

One folk tradition associated with the Nevern cross is that when St David travelled overland to Llanddewibrefi to address the synod on the threat of Palaganism he carried a cross on his back. He stopped midway to rest and swop halliluias with his friend Brynach Wyddel, the Irishman. When he resumed his journey David left the cross behind at Nevern. The story may in fact contain a residual of a folk memory to explain how the softer carboniferous sandstone from which the crosshead was carved, came from South Pembrokeshire. The fact that it makes such a clumsy fit with the hard dolerite module from which the shaft was carved is fairly obvious as is the crosshead on the Carew shaft. However since the Penally cross is all of piece perhaps what we can infer that the two crossheads, if not done by the same carver, may have been carved in a common workshop.

The Laugharne disc-head is framed by a heavy cable moulding within which is an equal-armed cross with a large central boss. Four triquetra knots fill the interspaces of the arms. The bottom arm has a large cable linking it with a running series of knots along the shaft of this small cross.

The Cross of Grutne in the Margam Museum is also small with the curving equal arms of the crosshead unadorned. There is a double circle in the centre of it. Sculpted from a single stone slab, the base below is entirely covered with a half-uncial inscription.

There are also a series of cross-slabs at Margam, in which the head has

Carew cross, Pembrokeshire. (Photograph by M.B.)

been carved in slight relief in the form of a spoked wheel at the top of the rectangular free-standing block. The central ringed boss has a series of eight equal triangles radiating outwards and surrounded by a double outer ring. The cross of Ilci is unadorned but with an inscription in the lined panel below. The cross of Iiquici is heavily decorated around the wheel. It has a large ringed boss in the centre. A faint inscription is on the shaft below. The reverse side has a double line at the centre of the wheel. Some decoration remains and there is a square equal-armed cross below it.

The cross of Confelyn is disc-headed. The ring of interlace contrasts a delicately carved plaitwork on the squared-off ends of a full-sized equal-armed cross. In the central square, the interlace around the central boss is wider on the right than on the left. The reverse side has weathered with the bottom half of a similar shaped cross decorated in fret and knot on the ring.

The disc-headed cross of Einon has a similar cross of decorated arms squared at the ends within a double ring. The pattern overlaps at the centre to enclose a 'rose' of knotted loop. The edges of both left and right arms have been shorn off indicating that the free-standing flat cross had been reused within Margam Abbey sometime after it was carved in the late ninth or early tenth-century. There are a number of other broken or smaller fragments of wheeled-crossheads as well as a six-spoked wheelhead and a slab with a Maltese cross in the museum.

The cross of Houelt at Llanilltud Fawr has a more pronounced disc-head than either of the above. Although slightly broken and incomplete at the neck, the decoration of the squared ring potent cross is an outstanding combination of large key patterned squares with smaller T-patterns linking the arms. The edges are slightly curved to fit neatly into the outer ring of interlace. Within the sunken interspaces are four triquetra knots shaped to fit neatly around the central square. An arrangement that also occurs on the east face of the Whitford wheelhead. The decoration on the reverse side is more weathered. The crosshead is formed by a similar square-ended cross potent but with the connecting links between the arms formed of paired frets.

The large 'Samson' stone slab is without a crosshead as is a smaller decorated slab in the old West church but it is probable that both had disc-heads like the cross of Houelt.

Wheelhead of pillar cross, St Roque's Chapel, Merthyr Mawr, Bridgend.

The ring and part of the crosshead of the 2.2m high Merthyr Mawr cross is broken. Originally both head and pillar-shaft were carved from one block of sandstone and it seems to have been one of the few examples (the Coychurch cross is another) of a true ringed cross in Wales. The cross originally stood in a field by the river but it was moved into the St Roque's chapel in the grounds of Merthyr Mawr House. A series of three-strand loops link together to decorate both side of the curving arms of the crosshead forming around the central boss. A decorative border is set above the panelled plinth. In the shelter behind the Merthyr Mawr church are a collection of decorated stones of various dates with a few weathered cart-wheeled type crosses and a Maltese cross set in a circular panelled slab.

The tall Coychurch cross, now in the corner of St Crallo's church, had stood outside until it was broken into three pieces by the falling church tower in 1877. The present base is undecorated but the remainder of shaft and head were carved, now very weathered. The splayed arms of the crosshead, without the enclosing ring, have triquetra knots linked around a central boss. Both faces have plain edge moulding and on the edges of the side arms are looped twists. The short stump of the neck has interlaced double-beaded knotwork. Another eleventh-century cross in Llandough churchyard, Penarth shows how ornate and baroque these tall Welsh crosses had become with its heavy moulded base, bulging columns beneath an over-hanging collar upon which the broken shaft stands. From a 1690 sketch by Lhwyd showing part of the head with a double-looped figure-of-eight design, it probably was a wheel-headed type crosshead on a shortened stump.

Broken wheelhead in Llangaffo Church, Anglesey.

In the porch of Llangaffo church on Anglesey is a lower part of an ornate wheelhead. The two remaining interspaces between the curved arms seem to have been actually pierced through. As we have seen, the 'true crosshead' so prevalent in Ireland, is not common on Welsh decorated high crosses so perhaps this is an example of a transitional phase of its development. The triple strands that are looped in a continuous ribbon-type decoration to form an equal-armed cross, with double circles in the centre representing the boss, are the same kind that form the interlace on one side of the Penmon shaft.

Two decorated wheelheads nestling in the window recesses of the north aisle of Llandeilo church in Carmarthenshire are the only evidence left of this once important clas dedicated to St Teilo. A squared equal-armed cross on both sides of one stone fragment is covered in a carved interlace pattern, set against a plain background. The carved strands run along the connecting arms and within the arms of one side are slightly raised bosses. This type of crosshead is similar to that on the cross of Houelt at Llanilltud Fawr although its decorated square arms are set on a ringed rather than the undecorated squared border here. The result makes one of the crosshead 'eared'. The other fragment has two different crosses carved on each side. On one is a variation of the squared cross with traces of decoration but on the other is a four-ringed equal-armed cross with large ringed studs in the interspaces. The design is surrounded by a double ring on the outside but without any other decoration.

Romilly Allen lists five different variations of the wheelhead that are particular to the cross in Wales. The overall form of the cross was altered by the shape of the arms, by the hollows between the arms, by combining the ends of the cross and ring, and by enlarging or contracting the depth of the ring.

There is the crosshead with square ends to arms, semi-circular or rounded hollows between the arms and combined with a circular ring as on the cross of Enniaun at Margam.

The crosshead with squared ends to arms, stepped hollows between arms, and combined with a circular ring as on the cross of Houelt or combined with a squared head as in Llandeilo church.

The crosshead with expanded ends to arms, semi-circular or round hollows between arms and combined with a circular ring as on the Carew cross.

The crosshead with no hollows between the arms and with slightly

Wheelhead in Llandeilo Church, Carmarthenshire;
and from the Cross of Einion, Margam, Port Talbot.

expanded arms beyond the enclosed circular ring as in the 'eared' cross at Penmon.

However if one examines the crossheads from all the existing crosses, as I have shown above, some observations can be made. The first is that very often the ornate Celtic patterns on the front and sides tend to obscure Allen's typology. Another is that in its physical presence, the cross seems less a combination of design quirks, more a work of art. Less cumbersome, lighter than reproductions on paper often suggest. And the stone cross adheres more to the visual or perceptual logic of a freestanding sculpture in space rather than illustrating a collection of Celtic patterns. It is often difficult to get close to the crosshead on top of a tall shaft and therefore hard to actually see the decoration.

Another curious effect is that the wheelhead tends to forget our definitions of a high cross. Height is often not the dominant aspect the term implies. At Margam Museum are a series of crosses on which the wheelhead has become the central feature of the shaft. The hollows that define the head of the Llanbadarn Fawr cross are merely extrusions of the narrow stone shaft with its heavily corded sides that seem to have been modelled or perhaps even copied from wood. At Merthyr Mawr, the fragmented wheelhead sits on what appears to have been an enlarged plinth. On the wonderfully decorated cross of Confelyn, its small shaft was made even shorter, sometime in the past. The effect is that of the overwrought wheelhead contracting into the rounded base. It is not an unattractive cross, in fact the opposite, but it should make one aware of the variable definitions of the high cross as a decorated three-dimensional religious object carved to be seen, prayed to, touched and venerated within the confines of a churchyard.

Decorated Pedestals

The block on the stone base in Llangyfelach churchyard has a succinct modern inscription in Roman capitals. BASE/OF ANCIENT/ CHURCHYARD/CROSS DATE/TENTH CENTURY. It tells us all we think we need to know about how the cross remained upright for the stone itself appears substantial and roughly hewn in contrast to the slightly curving pedestal. In fact this is a recent stone covering to protect the actual socket which measures 48 x 30 x 33cm deep. Rectangular in shape – 114 x 58 x 76cm high – with about half of the block's present depth originally set into the ground. Four sides are decorated with bands of fret and knotwork and the main oblong knot on the north face has pellets protruding in each loop. It was carved to fit the slightly lopsided stone with a two-band knot that turns into a triple band at the other end. It is touches like this that show us the working craft of the mason by fitting a preconceived pattern into the actual shape of the material. The imperfections within the perfect ordering of Celtic art that reflects the divine nature of the Lord of creation.

Pedestal in Llangyfelach churchyard, Swansea.

Two other crosses from Glamorgan, the Llandough and the Confelyn at Margam, have such a base for seating the shaft on. The latter has three sides decorated with fret and plaitwork and a hunting scene carved on its east face. Around a rider with a shield are the prey and what may be his retinue. The top of the actual base is decorated with a fine display of double knotwork that begins on one corner and continues around the socket to become a three-corded plait and end again in double knots. The west side of the base of the Llandough cross also has a horse and rider by a spiral loop and with a series of interlocked rings set beneath the belly and between the legs of the horse. It is clearly separate and must have had some symbolic meaning to the carver of the pedestal.

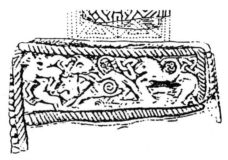

Base of the Cross of Confelyn, Margam, Port Talbot.

On the east side is a group of five seated ecclesiastical? figures with staffs and on each of the other ends are busts of a man. Sutton stone used for the base is now quite weathered so their relation to the cross or who they may have originally represented is lost to us. However the cast in the National Museum of Wales has been painted, as has the broken shaft from Penally, which helps to bring out the scene into relief. This was done as an experiment to show what is understood as the final phase in the making of a stone cross although admitting that all traces of such paint have generally now weathered away.

Do we need to accept such decorative aids as the sine qua non of the medieval carver? An artist whose art would have been transcendental in the highest sense of what the cross of Christ – no matter what medium was used – meant to ecclesiastics and laity alike. Some stone crosses may have had paint applied to them in later centuries for as the fourteenth-century wall paintings in St Illtud's church at Llanilltud Fawr show, such decoration added a richness to the stone interiors of pre-Reformation churches.

A curious elaboration of the cross base is evident in a number of pieces from this area in which the elongated pedestal takes the place of an actual shaft but probably holding a short ringed crosshead as in the slab cross of Merthyr Mawr. The ornate pedestals here, at Margam and Llanilltud Fawr may indicate a particular development of the plinth-cross within a local workshop. The actual form without any decoration brings to mind the shape of the altar found near the Roman fort at Laugher. It is at present in the Swansea Museum. The carving of an Irish Ogam inscription on one edge shows that it may have been used during the immediate post-Roman period in a different ritual context.

Inscribed shaft (of unknown cross) in St Crallo's Church, Coychurch, Bridgend.

The font at the end of the nave of Penmon Church, discovered in a stonemasons yard in Beaumaris in the last century, was once the base of a cross whose whereabouts are unknown. It is decorated on three sides with bold variations on the key or T-fret pattern. The high cross that was in the Deer Park is mounted on a very weathered truncated base which was carved in a series of strong geometrical designs. The illustrations by Westwood show the front to have been a double squared maze running

Five-sided pedestal (of unknown cross) in the church porch, Dyserth, Flintshire.

Freestanding cross, Penmon, Anglesey.

in opposite ways and the back had over fifty reticulated small squares that splayed out from 27 to 35 inches at the bottom by 21 inches high. In many ways the decoration on this base seems more in keeping with the almost total geometric designs on the other free-standing cross which is mounted in a modern block nearby, although Nash-Williams thought that the font may have been its original base.

In the church porch at Dyserth in Flintshire is an unattached base that may have belonged to a freestanding cross that cannot now be located. An illustration by Westwood showing a smaller almost baroque cross between the front and back views of the tall freestanding cross with a fractured crosshead that stands in the churchyard, may have been the shaft. The base is truncated with three sloping sides to the front carved with ring crosses and a three-strand loop while the long back part shows a ring cross amid some decoration.

The tall freestanding cross in Flintshire which is known as Maen Achwyfan is mounted in a sunken square slab. Early illustrations show some suggestive 'arrow' marks on the stone base. At Corwen in Denbighshire the tall shaft of the twelfth-century churchyard cross is set

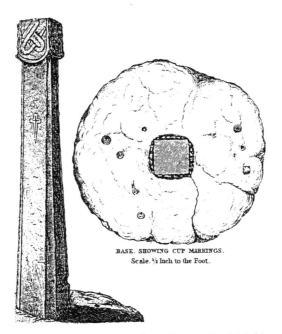

BASE. SHOWING CUP MARKINGS.
Scale. ½ Inch to the Foot.

Churchyard cross with stone base, Corwen, Denbighshire.

in a circular stone 1.7m across and 0.3m high. On the visible upper surface are seven cupmarks. There are also two small Latin crosses set in relief on the shaft, the top of which has four inverted curves and some interlacing similar to on the Pillar of Eliseg which stands near the ruined abbey of Valle Crucis, Llangollen.

If the large ring motif on the shafts of the Penmon crosses was influenced by the Manx crosses; and the crosshead so obviously a Northern type; then the panels of elongated knotwork, the figure of St Anthony on the front and the decorated bases are rooted in the Irish high-cross tradition. Especially if the designs on the pedestals are seen as part of a pictorial whole. And perhaps even symbolically in the manner that the base, shaft and ringed crosshead were thought to encapsulate the steps, church and the cross that Constantine erected on Golgotha 'Place of the Skull' where Christ was put to death. In the writings of Adamnan, the ninth abbot of Iona who died in 704, there is a description of the Church of the Holy Sepulchre. Below its domed roof was a great silver cross set in the same socket as the original wooden cross of Christ. His informant, a Bishop Arculf who had lived in Jerusalem for nine months, even drew a sketch of the church.

Anglesey may have been an important melting pot in this respect and even with a large sculpture workshop addressing local needs. Along with the Penmon collection there are stone fragments as well as the broken crosshead at Llangabbo and even later (Group 11) cross-slabs showing outlined Latin crosses with pointed ends and including spiral decoration. Among the many important church sites and crosses is the seventh-century Cadfan stone in the north wall of Llangadwaladr church and the later medieval sculpture carvings in Llanbabo church, showing the legendary king Pabo, and the Evan stone now in the Bangor Museum.

The hunting scene on the pedestal of the Confelyn cross and horseman on the Llandough base may have been influenced by the number of similar scenes that are a feature of the bases on some the most well known high crosses in the eastern region of Ireland. A hunting scene on both E and W faces of the base of the Cross of Patrick and Columba at Kells and on the base of the Castledermot cross. Horsemen are on the E and W faces of the base of the south cross at Clonmacnois and on the S face of the Cross of the Scriptures; on the E base of the Kells Market cross and on the S base of the Cross of Muiredach at Monasterboice Co. Louth.

Equally the use of abstract designs on the Penmon bases, on the Llangyfelach base and on the Confelyn pedestal can be duplicated on these and on other crosses throughout Ireland.

Memorial Inscriptions

A common feature on many Welsh stone crosses is the memorial dedication to a king or personage of social standing. The practice of inscribing large flatish stones goes back to the Roman occupation when gravemarkers and roadstones were common. The large triangular stone from Llantrisant in Anglesey in even cut lettering mourns a most holy woman who lies there, the loving wife of Bavatigimus, servant of God, a bishop. Other stones record two priests at Capel Anelog, near Aberdaron; a doctor on the Melus stone at Llangian; a citizen of Venedos who was also a cousin of Maglos the magistrate at Penmachno; as well as the more well known one to 'Carausius (who) lies here in this heap of stones', with the early Christian *Chi-Rho* monogram carved over it from the 6th century.

During the Dark Ages the commemorative formulas became somewhat modified but the graveside message continued as a mark of popular respect to the dead leader. Since the names of some known Welsh kings have been recorded in this manner it is possible to date the inscriptions fairly precisely. The silent memorial stone can thus be read as a significant historical document as well as being a time-key to other stones with similar lettering. It must always be borne in mind that the more usual forms of written historical material in medieval Wales are almost non-existent until around the Norman period.

The stone set in the north wall of the church at Llangadwaladr in Anglesey commemorates King Cadamanus, Cadfan in Welsh, ruler of the kingdom of Gwynedd who died early in the 7th century. His son Cadwallon was killed in 634 and his grandson Cadwaladr (+664) was the traditional founder of this church. Carved horizontally in four lines of mainly half-uncial letters and set beneath an incised Latin cross, the grand eulogy to Cadfan describes him as the wisest and most renowned of all kings.

Cadfan stone, Llangadwaladr Church, Anglesey. (Drawing by M.H.)

Nash-Williams suggests the lettering includes Roman capitals and points out that the A and the variants of M (looking like double h's) are used in the *Book of Kells*. In fact nearly all the letterforms used can be found in that illuminated manuscript which is thought to have begun on Iona in the early eighth-century and brought to the monastery at Kells in the mid-700's. The carving certainly suggests an Irish influence based on the use of the manuscript hand. Being found on an early church site may also indicate the liminal separation between the sacred enclosure of the burial ground and the royal court at Aberffraw across the river Gwna.

The 31 lines of Latin text recorded by Edward Lhwyd in 1696 on the Pillar of Eliseg is a more grandiloquent testimonial of kingly power. The cross was a local landmark before it was thrown over during the Civil War hence the name of the valley and the ruined Cistercian abbey of Valle Crucis. In 1779, the remaining two parts of the pillarstone were placed on the tumulus where it now stands. The inscription is almost indistinct but from Lhwyd's notes we learn that '+ whomsoever/shall read this hand-inscribed stone let him give a blessing on/the soul of Eliseg + it is Conceann . . .' and further down that it was Conmarch who inscribed the pillar.

Ruler of the kingdom of Powys, Concenn died on a pilgrimage in Rome in 854. He was the great grandson of King Eliseg who was killed fighting the Saxons. A letter, now in Rome, written by an Irish cleric to his teacher mentions Concenn. It gives us a glimpse of the Celtic notions of honour and of keeping face; of the pilgrim route across Britain at this time; and perhaps a deeper meaning behind some of these inscriptions in terms of riddles and conundrums. The letter begins: Please understand, wise and estimable Colgan, our very learned teacher, that we are not transmitting this exposition to you as to one needing such enlightenment, but we humbly ask that in your kindness you would give this information to such of our simple and unsophisticated Irish brethren as may think of sailing across the British Sea, lest perchance otherwise they may be made to blush in the presence of Merfyn, the glorious King of the Britons, at not being able to understand that inscription. One of the chief druids in the court was in the habit of testing the learned mettle of Irish pilgrims by asking them to decipher an inscription which would guarantee their safe passage across Powys. It was 'King Merfyn greets Concenn' his brother-in-law. (Chadwick, 1959)

In the church of Llandyfaelog fach, a few miles north of Brecon, a tall and quite narrow slab-cross shows a figure in a tunic with a spear and a dagger. He is surrounded and outlined by interlace and fret border. On the panel above is a Latin cross formed of double bands that are looped at the end of the arms and upright. A series of triquerta knots fill the interspaces at the top and below the arms of the cross. On the plain panel below this kingly figure is an inscription in half-uncial lettering +briamail/flou. The name is almost like the 'Brohcmail' named on the pillar above as the son of Eliseg.

The ruler of Glywysing, a kingdom in the south-east between the River Tawe and the Usk (roughly modern Glamorgan) is commemorated on the imposing disc-headed cross standing in the West Church of

Detail of cross-slab,
Llandyfaelog fach, Powys.

Detail of Cross of Houelt,
Llanilltud Fawr, Vale of Glamorgan.

Llanilltud Fawr. The Latin inscription in five lines of half-uncial script without punctuation or letter spacing invokes the Name of God the Father and of the Son and of the Holy Spirit Houelt prepared this cross for the soul of Res his father. Rhys and his son Hywel ap Rhys probably ruled middle to end of the ninth century to which the cross has been dated.

Another stone here known as the Pillar of Samson which is nearly 3m tall has a long Latin inscription reading: 'In the name of the most high God begins the cross/of the Saviour which Samson/the Abbot prepared for his soul and for the soul/of Iuthahelo the King and of Artmail and of Tecan'. The king named here is thought to be Ithel of Gwent who died in 846.

Llanilltud Fawr, the great church of Illtud, is the original of the crass English name *Llantwit Major*. Abbot Samson who is also named on another pillar stone shows that it was a Celtic rather than a Roman monastic centre, a Bangor that traditionally was the greatest college in pre-Norman Wales. Royal burials in the old church, the site of the present West Church, are yet another indication of its spiritual power and

Samson's Cross, Llanilltud Fawr, Vale of Glamorgan.

temporal influence. The decoration on the front of the free-standing pillar which is without its original crosshead, has weathered but compared to its ordered panels of fine carved knotwork and t-fret patterns the half-uncial inscriptions are untidy and loose. Probably done by a different hand from the mason who carved the cross leaving two blank panels in front. The Latin message is spread over both. +Samson placed his cross for his soul+'. The reverse has four names +Illtud+Samson the king Samuel+Ebisar+ with the sign of the cross set in four small panels.

Ralegh Radford's 1949 interpretation of the jumbled letters on one of the two front panels of the Carew cross is in keeping with the notion of the high cross as a royal memorial. As well as being historically credible it also more importantly gives a probable date and occasion for erecting it. O.S. Westwood, John Rhys and others had put forward ingenious readings but Radford's rearrangement was 'margit/eut/re/x etg (um) filius' which he translated as Margiteut (or Maredudd) son of Etguin (or Edwin). With his brother Hywel, Maredudd ap Edwin was joint ruler of the south-western kingdom of Deheubarth until he was killed in 1035. If this was indeed a cross commissioned by Hywel, and it seems to be now generally accepted as such without question, the other panel remained forever blank.

Rubbing (quarter-size) of inscription on Carew cross. (Photograph by M.H.)

Rubbing (quarter-size) of inscription on Nevern cross. (Photograph by M.H.)

Rubbing (quarter-size) of inscription on Nevern cross. (Photograph by M.H.)

Richard Fenton in 1809, saw in Nevern churchyard, 'one of these early crosses, consisting of a tall shaft similar to that represented as standing in front of Carew Castle but more elegantly wrought, having a small compartment amidst the carved work. It is ornamented with, some strange characters, which I have not heard were ever deciphered, no more than that at Carew'.

The equally obscure inscription on a panel of the east face, a jumble of h-a.-e-n-h. does not appear to have roused the same interest as on the Carew cross. However R.A.S. Macalister, the Irish scholar and epigrapher who published his Corpus (of the Inscriptions of the Insular Celts) in 1945 suggested that it might be an abbreviation from the Greek of 'halliluia'. Coupled with the Latin d n s on the west face, an abbreviation of dominus, Lord, it might seem that the inscriptions were carved to show off the learned religious tone of this ancient clas of St Brynach. Compared to the above inscriptions and to the majority on other Welsh crosses of single names or brief injunction as 'Moridic raised this stone', the Nevern ones seem almost non-conformist in their brevity and adoration of the Lord.

References

(The High Cross)
Davies, W.; *Wales in the Early Middle Ages* (Leicester, 1982).
Macalister, R.A.S.; *Corpus Inscriptionum Insularum Celticarum* (Dublin, 1945).
RCAHMW, Glamorgan. Vol.1 Part III (HMSO, Cardiff, 1976).
Henry, F.; *Early Christian Irish Art* (Cork, 1979).
Richardson, H. & Scarry, J.; *Irish High Crosses* (Dublin, 1990).
Redknap, M.; *The Christian Celts* (NMW, Cardiff, 1991).
Davies, J.L. & Kirby, D.P. (Eds.); *Cardiganshire County History* Vol.1 (Cardiff, 1994).
Rynne, E. (Ed.); *Figures from the Past* (Dublin, 1987).
Ryan, M. (Ed.); *Ireland and Insular Art AD500-1200* (RIA, Dublin, 1987).
Borne, C. (Ed.); *From the Isles of the North* (HMSO, Belfast, 1995).
Kelly, D.; *Irish High Crosses*, JRSAI Vol. 116 (Dublin, 1956).
Lang, J.; *Anglo-Saxon Sculpture* (Aylesbury, 1988).

(Free-standing Monuments)
Giraldus Cambrensis; *The Itinerary Through Wales and the Description of Wales* (London, 1903).
Edwards, N.; *11th-Century Welsh Illuminated Manuscripts*, in Borne, E. (Ed.); *From the Isles of the North* (ibid.)
Bowen, E.C.; *Saints, Seaways and Settlements* (Cardiff, 1977).
Allen, J.R.; *The Early Christian Monuments of Scotland* (Edinburgh, 1903).
Nash-Williams, V.E.; *The Early Christian Monuments of Wales* (Cardiff, 1950).
James, H.; *Excavations at Caer, Bayvil*, in Edwards, N. & Lane, A. (Eds); *The Early Church in Wales and the West* (Cardiff, 1992).
Allen, J.R.; *Celtic Art* (Studio Editions, London, 1993).
Allen, J.R.; *Celtic Crosses of Wales* (Felinfach, Dyfed, 1989).
Davies, W.; *Wales in the Early Middle Ages* (ibid.).
Crawford, H.S.; *Irish Carved Ornament* (Cork, 1980).
O hEailidhe, P.; *The Cross-Base at Oldcourt*, in Rynne, E. (Ed.); *Figures from the Past* (ibid.)
Bailey, R.N.; *Viking Age Sculpture in Northern England* (London, 1980).

(Cross within a Cross)
Allen, J.R.; *Celtic Crosses of Wales* (ibid).

(Decorated Pedestals)
Redknap, M.; *The Christian Celts* (ibid.)
Lang, J.; *Anglo-Saxon Sculpture* (ibid.)
Owen, E.; *Old Stone Crosses in the Vale of Clwyd* (London, 1886).
Richardson, H. & Scarry, J.; *Irish High Crosses* (ibid.)

(Memorial Inscriptions)
Bain, G.; *Celtic Art, The Methods of Construction* (Glasgow, 1945).
Chadwick, H.M. (Ed.); *Studies in the Early British Church* (Cambridge, 1959).
Radford, R.; *The Carew Cross* (Arch. Camb., 1969).
Fenton, R.; *A Historical Tour through Pembrokeshire* (Reprinted 1903).

Cross in St Martin's Church, Laugharne, Carmarthenshire.
(Photograph by M.H.)

Part 3

A Journey Around Wales

Viewing the High Crosses

Visiting Welsh museums could be an off-putting business for the serious searcher. Their opening hours, the no-touch policy, idiosyncratic lighting and the way monuments were displayed was often confusing. But that has changed now with the more 'educational' backgrounds generally on view. Passing Margam Abbey on the M4 I decided on the spur of the moment to revisit the small airless building they grandly call the Stones Museum. The Old School House was locked. When I enquired in the cafe, was told that as a reconstruction was underway, the crosses were stored elsewhere. This had been going on for over a year and Cadw had given no indication when they might be seen again. All part of the trend to make every monument part of the heritage industry.

Earlier in the year Swansea Museum was also under reconstruction. However, I was fortunate to find the stone fragment from Coelbren under a staircase, along with the Roman altar from Lougher. The slab with the orans figure in a skirt is bigger, more impressive than reproduction suggests. In the National Museum at Cardiff the large-scale collection of casts from the most important high crosses in Wales are on display in the upper permanent gallery. Mixed in with a number of actual early Christian stone monuments, they are embedded in a tiered tableau and surrounded by small stones to suggest a sort of memorial garden.

In 1990 I tried unsuccessfully to get permission to take rubbings of some for an exhibition in Cardigan. Later when I met Mark Redknap the Assistant Keeper he maintained that they had a public duty to protect the monuments. When I pointed out that much of the display were of casts, he informed me that even the casts were now classed as ancient monuments and as member of the public I was not allowed to handle them. Other museums were more flexible and are extremely helpful in regard to rubbings. It is often overlooked in relation to carved crosses that an original reproduction done with care is much better for their study than even the best of photographs. For one thing the actual size and even the imperfections of individual panels show up on paper. In relation to their height and width, it is often impossible to get even an approximation of scale from a photograph. Standing in front of a tall stone cross, the human eye compresses it into our individual field of vision so that close-to even the panels appear to be smaller than they in fact are. This can be tested quite simply by taking a rubbing and then holding the paper in your hands which seems to be so much bigger than the carving itself.

A few of the crosses remain in situ. They may help to remind us that the original placement in the southside of the churchyard was a religious act that gave meaning to the symbolism of the carved cross. So when removed from the ground and placed inside the church, as were many for reasons of safety, the cross begins to lose its intrinsic power. It is an old notion, but many like myself, still believe that the actual spot associated with the placement of a stone or cross was especially sacred because it marked and represented a confluence of natural and psychic elements. So without its exposure to the daily movement of the sun, wind and rain the cycle of surface decay by licken is aborted. The geomagnetic flows and the water currents below ground no longer condition the stone. And most of all the sympathetic magic or feeling that people gave to it by way of veneration, praying and touching the cross ceased when taken from its original environment.

So by the time it is placed inside the air-conditioned surroundings of a modern museum, it becomes something to be looked at. A piece of heritage! As a decorative object the original carving has little more worth than a replica. And for purposes of study an exact cast copy done many years ago may be better for as is evident from the Penally cross the damp conditions inside the church caused some damage to the surface decoration.

In fact, when commissioned by the curator of the Aberystwyth Museum to do a full-size cloth rubbing of the Padarn Cross for display in the new E.G. Bowen extension showing the history of the area from the prehistoric to the medieval, I wondered about the necessity of such an inclusion when the real cross was on view in the church itself less than half-a-mile away from the town centre.

However, when completed with the cloth stretched on a wooden replica standing against the wall, it showed the front and both sides of the ten feet high cross much more clearly than the original weathered stone. The rubbing on unbleached calico using coloured waxes was highlighted by the application of some earth and grass from outside the church. A practice that adds a little something from the immediate area of a stone cross. In a sense giving back some of the natural environment for this cross was moved inside the Llanbadarn Fawr church in 1916 in order to prevent further damage 'at the hands of ignorant visitors and others'. Apart from the natural weathering it is hard to see what kind of damage had been inflicted beforehand. Inside the church it still suffers from the tactile impulse to run one's hands along the curves of this ancient stone. The current trend in the preservation of Irish high crosses at Clonmacnois and elsewhere is not only to remove the original inside the newly-constructed interpretative centre but to replace it with a full-scale reproduction in position where the stone cross once stood. Thereby not only confusing the casual visitor but conflating reality with fantasy in a curious attempt to deny or at least slow down the processes of change and decay.

As well as the museums mentioned above, Bangor, Carmarthen and Brecon have small displays of carved stones and local crosses from the Roman period on. The tableau in the latter includes the delicately decorated Llanynys pillar cross with its corded sides showing clearly the wooden or metal prototype on which it was modelled. There is also a cast of the Llywel stone from Trecastle which is now in the British Museum. On the hidden side of this large slab is a single cupmark and a dual inscription in Latin and Ogam. On the face showing is probably the most curious of all the inscribed stones in Wales. It shows a number of 'stick' figures surrounded by cross symbols and since one has what may be a crosier it is generally thought to have been carved later during the Christian period. The cross slab of Moridic in Llanhamlach church a few miles from Brecon also has similar crude figuration. It is one of a number of decorated stones in churches within the immediate locality. The general policy now with such Welsh monuments is to leave the stone crosses in the relative safety of the churches where they have been placed during the past half-century.

The problem is finding a key or someone who knows where it might be for most churches are now locked during the week. This is an understandable precaution in view of the scale of ecclesiastical losses through theft. However it is annoying after making an expensive and time consuming journey to Penmon church during the off-season and failing to gain entrance. Finding the locations in Ceredigion of the decorative fragments or the crosses in small churches spread throughout mid Wales can be a major undertaking.

There are always compensations! The wall paintings in St Illtud's Church Llanilltud Fawr that still survive from the thirteenth century give a much greater sense of the late medieval church than even the Houelt Cross which stands inside the West Church. Built on the site of the old Celtic setting it now houses a fine collection of decorated stones and later medieval effigies. Like the Merthyr Mawr collection, also in the Vale of Glamorgan, these are virtual specialist museums. The equally picturesque church of St Brynach in Nevern, Pembrokeshire, has a number of crosses and some early inscribed stones that date from the sixth century. Along with the detailed guide books, postcards and background information these churches combine the sense of a living religious faith with the preservation of the Christian legacy from an era long before the present stone churches were built. At Llanwnda, further down the same coast past Fishguard towards Strumble Head, a small church dedicated to St Gwyndal has an interesting collection of uninscribed cross-slabs embedded in the outside walls. On a window sill inside the eastern end is a stone fragment with a figure of a cleric about nine inches high holding a staff in one hand with the other raised in benediction. The robes are curved in a distinctive manner, the folding suggestive of late medieval effigy sculpture.

Its miniature quality brings to mind the small Celtic cross in St Martin's at Laugharne on the other side of the peninsula, by Carmarthen Bay. It is barely two feet high with a moulded equal-armed crosshead that is linked in relief by a thick cable plait that forms the shaft itself. It is now set in a niche in the transept wall of this extremely large ornate parish church.

The Penally cross-shaft has suffered extensive fragmentation of the decorated surface due to the damp and rather airless conditions of St Nicholas Church. The shaft stands in the south transet close to the wall. It was discovered in 1851 under a raised gallery that then stood at the western end and was found to be mortised at the top for a crosshead.

Edward Laws in *Little England Beyond Wales*, published in 1888, bemoaned the amount of shaling on the carving, the extent can be gauged when comparing the drawing in O.S. Westwood's *Lapidarium Walliae* with its present condition. Recently parts of the decorated surface of the heavy corded knotwork above the motif of the 'confronting beasts' have been cemented back onto the sandstone pillar. It now stands on one side of the painted glass window with the cross on the either side, in the south transept. A large niche in the eastern wall holds a long cross-decorated medieval slab. The new red carpeting with the altar table and the surrounding crosses, even the installation of a light switch on the pew by which one can contemplate the stone relics, are all part of the current trend to make the monuments more accessible to visitors. The uneven sandstone plinth on which the cross once stood can still be seen amid the gravestones outside the door of the churchtower.

Base of Penally cross, St Nicholas churchyard, Penally, Pembrokeshire.
(Photograph by M.H.)

Descriptive Survey of Early Medieval Monuments

Note:

Entries in the guide are arranged according to the 1996 Welsh Unitary boundaries. In many ways this has facilitated what was standard archaeological practice in using the names of the old countries prior to the 1974 reformed seven counties in place of the previous thirteen. Thus Anglesey has become a region in its own right. Ceredigion (old Cardiganshire), Pembrokeshire and Carmarthenshire replace Dyfed. Bridgend is West Glamorgan and South and Mid are now the Vale of Glamorgan. Cardiff and Newport replace Gwent. Brecon is in a new region of Powys, Clwyd has been replaced by the old areas of Flintshire and Denbighshire. The guide begins at Penmon in Anglesey and follows this geographical route around Wales to end at the Whitford high cross in Flintshire.

The following abbreviations are used in reference.

ECMW	Early Christian Monuments of Wales by V. Nash-Williams, Cardiff, 1950.
CADW - CP	A Guide to Ancient and Historic Wales – Clwyd and Powys by Helen Burnham (HMSO 1995).
CADW - D	A Guide to Ancient and Historic Wales – Dyfed, by Sian Rees (HMSO 1992).
CADW - G	A Guide to Ancient and Historic Wales – Gwynedd, by Frances Lynch (HMSO, 1995).
CADW - GG	A Guide to Ancient and Historic Wales – Glamorgan and Gwent by Elisabeth Whittle (HMSO, 1992).
CCH	Cardiganshire County History, Vol. 1 by J.L. Davies and D.P. Kirby (Eds.) (Cardiff, 1994).
CIIC	Corpus Inscriptionum Insularum Celticarum, by R.A.S. Macalister (Dublin, 1945).
RCAHMW	Royal Commission on Ancient and Historical Monuments, in Wales. Glamorgan Volume 1, Part 3 (HMSO, 1976)
OS	Ordnance Survey number for the appropriate 1:50,000 map.

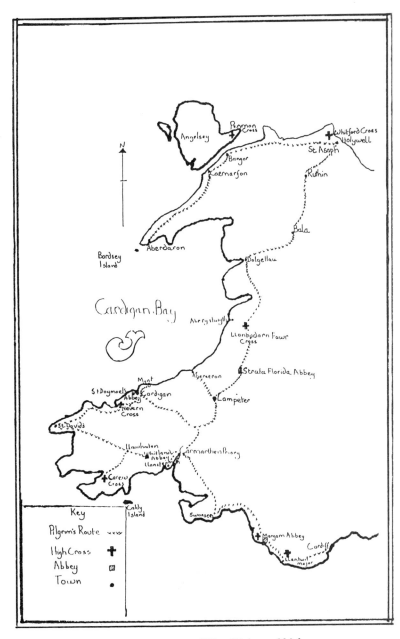

Medieval pilgrim routes of West Wales and high crosses.

Anglesey

FREESTANDING CROSS, Penmon Church, Penmon, 4 miles north-east of Beaumaris

The Penmon Cross stood for many years in the Deer Park but it is now in the nave of the priory church, part of the old Priory with the lodging-private house – and the remains of the refectory. Nearby is a much later dovecote. The cross was a composite work with the decorated shaft 1.8m high actually tenoned at both ends to be mounted on a truncated base and fitted into the mortice on the underside of the fractured crosshead. It has lost most of its original carving and is now very weathered. Nash-Williams described it as 'eared', the slight protruding arms outside the ringhead being a local type.

On the front of the shaft, the central panel showed animal headed demons on both sides of a robed and haloed figure. It probably represented the Temptation of St Anthony in the desert. Above and below the saint are interlaced panels divided by narrow inset bands. At the bottom is a figure on horseback with animals. Five bold chain-ring vertical loops cover the back of the shaft. This motif is a characteristic one in the Isle of Man, especially on the cross-slabs carved by Gaut around the 950's. The Penmon Cross has been dated slightly later to the end of 10th century.

Freestanding cross, Penmon, Anglesey.

A double-T fret design runs up on the right face of the shaft with a double strand and then a triple loop which is continued down the left face to end in a scene of a human figure with four animals. One has its legs in the air! The decoration on the shaft is in low relief, similar to that on the 2ft high rectangular weathered pedestal. Its front had four square fret patterns, on the back is a wheel-cross and on the others sides, a large reticulated pattern of raised dots and vestiges of plain plaitwork.

Refs. ECMW No. 38; CADW-G No. 103; OS No. SH 630807.

CROSS-SLAB. Penmon Church, Penmon, 4 miles north-east of Beaumaris.

In the south transept of the church is a 2m high cross that had been used as a lintel for the window of the refectory thereby losing one of the arms of its eared-disc crosshead. It shows a plain carved ring cross with splaying arms. Four triguetra-knots decorate the interspaces. The reverse is much the same with one side fractured away. The shaft is sculpted on all sides with fret patterns arranged vertically but broken by knotwork on both front and back. On the left side the fret ends as an animal-headed demon and centre right is a small bird form.

The cross is set in a modern brick base. However the original pedestal may be the decorated stone font once used in Beaumaris Church after being found in a stonemason's yard during the last century. The decoration on the font at the end of the nave is a squared fret-pattern on three of its sides.

Inside the refectory is another freestanding slab of similar shape and size but it is extremely weathered and without obvious decoration. In the outside wall above the window, to the side of the porch, is a smaller worn cross showing two hollows from the interspaces of the arms.

It was Elian who established the cell and healing well at Penmon in the sixth century. He placed his nephew Seiriol in charge so that the monastery subsequently became known as the 'saintly congregation of Seiriol'. The abbey church, 'the most complete 12th century structure in Anglesey' (CADW Guide), was built during the reign of Owain Gwynedd and eventually became an Augustinian priory. It was dissolved at the Reformation. With its substantial buildings, high crosses, renowned holy spring and saint's bed in the rockface behind the church, the early medieval monastery was an important pilgrimage centre. The founder's hermitage on Puffin Island, formally Priestholm or Priest's island was known as Ynys Seiriol.

Refs. ECMW No. 37, 1; CADW-G No. 103: OS No. SH 630807.

WHEELHEAD, Llangaffo Church, 1 mile north-east of Newborough.

In the porch is the lower half of an ornate wheelhead. The two remaining interspaces between the carved arms are actually pierced through. The crosshead appears to have been formed by triple strands looped in a continuous ribbon-style decoration to form an equal-armed cross. There is a double circle in the centre to represent the boss, a feature that linked the four outer hollows within the moulding. The extremely bold design of this fragment with its tenon below to sit into the shaft of a freestanding cross would have been visually striking in the old churchyard prior to the demolition of the old church and the building of the present nondescript one. Near the old foundations are some broken bits of a pillar cross, with a splayed decorated shaft over two feet high and a smaller stone fragment. The decoration on the former included a carved wheel-cross and some bands of plaitwork and T-fretwork. On the latter stone some plaitwork and a quadrupled triangular panel are present.

Broken wheelhead, Llangaffo Church, Anglesey.

Llangaffo was an important early Christian site dedicated to St Cabbo, a brother to Gildas the Wise. Built into the churchyard wall are late small stone slabs with incised Latin-type crosses. Their pointed ends perhaps illustrating the metal or wood crosses that could have been pushed into the ground prior to the more general use of stone memorials. In the sacristy is a 7th century inscribed stone carved in upper and lowercase lettering that has been read as 'Gvernin son of Couris Cini set up this stone', a formula that is common on some of the south Wales crosses. *Ref. ECMW No. 14, 15, 16; CADW-G No. 102; OS No. SH 446685.*

Ceredigion

PILLAR CROSS, St Padarn Church, Llanbadarn Fawr, Aberystwyth.

The cross set inside the south transept of the church is among a handful of the most impressive freestanding crosses in Wales. According to Samuel Rush Meyrick (*History & Antiquities of the County of Cardigan, 1810*) it stood in a 'reclining posture, having fallen from its original situation which was perpendicular. It is 7ft 8ins in height above ground'. Moved from its original south-west aspect between the nave and transept nearer to the church in 1840, it was brought inside fifty years later in order, according to the memorandum to the Royal Commission on Ancient Monuments, 'to prevent further damage at the hands of ignorant visitors and others'. It still looks as worn as old wood!

The squared narrow monolith (3m high) is sculpted on all sides from the top of its cross-head to the bottom of the shaft where a triple spiral was discovered when it was lifted from the ground in 1916. The four deep hollows that define the crosshead appear to have been scalloped from the top of the pillar. It is now very weathered but from J.O. Westwood (*Lapidarium Walliae*) it is clear that the ribbon interlace formed a cross around the central boss on the rear side, much in the manner of the Llanynnis cross in Powys. The decoration continues into the topmost panel. In the fourth panel down this motif changes into a beast eating its tail, below which is a section of t-fret ornament and a triple spiral carved at the bottom of the pillar. Ribbon decoration runs the length of one side and the key-or-fret pattern of the wheelhead is repeated on the other side within the heavily corded edges.

The original block of stone is thought to have been hewn in the Llŷn peninsula. Close examination of the cross shows that the four sides, each

Detail of cross, Llanbadarn Fawr, Ceredigion. (Photograph by M.B.)

measuring less than eleven inches wide, are 'out-of-true' on the perpendicular. An indication perhaps that the carver was working up from a wooden model probably smaller in length than the finished cross. Its corded edges are also indicative of a wooden prototype. It would be fanciful to suppose that it may have been the staff or holy relic that in the Life of St Padarn was given to him as a gift by the Patriarch of Jerusalem. The seated figure in the largest panel on the front of the cross with swept-back ringulated hair may represent Christ in Majesty or saint Padarn as episcopal head of Llanbadarn.

The Padarn cross is at present set into a white marbled floor in the south transept of the church as the centrepiece of an exhibition of stained glass and illustrations showing the development of the site from its 6th century founder to the period when the church was pre-eminent in medieval Wales.

Ref. ECMW No. 111; CCH No. 28; CADW-D No. 104; OS SN 599810.

CROSS-SLAB, Llanwnnws Church, Ystrad Meurig, 5 miles north of Tregaron.

The carving in low relief of ribbon terminal knots and ring bosses in the interspaces of the cross shows a transition from the simple inscribed Latin cross to a more ornate style. The stem in ribbon form ends in a Stafford knot and a smaller one survives on the right arm beyond the double corded ring. The letters XPS (Christos) may have been matched on the left with IHS (Jesus) as common contractions derived from Greek letters. Another local example is on the Gurmarc stone in St David's cathedral. The 1.4m high slab, dated to the late eighth-century, has an inscription alongside and below the cross in half-uncial letters.

Ref. ECMW No. 125; CCH No. 22; CADW-D No. 102; CIIC No. 994; OS SN 685696.

STONE SLAB, Silian Church, 2 miles north of Lampeter.

In the vestry is a rectangular slab with both faces carved in the Celtic manner of decoration. On the top of one side is a pattern of six interlinked knots and on the other is a squared fret motif. Both are similar in certain respects to panels on the Nevern Cross and may have been carried out as trial carvings for the larger work. An identical carving of six large interlocking knots can be seen in the porch of Llanilar church, 5 miles south-east of Aberystwyth. Until recently it was at the nearby

Rubbing (one-tenth) of decorated slab, Silian Church, Ceredigion.

Castle Hill house but it originally came from an earthwork at Cribyn, much nearer in fact to Silian.

Ref. ECMW No. 128, 129; CCH No. 34, 32; CADW-D No. 100, 103; OS SN 572513 & 624751.

STONE SLABS, Llanddewi Church, Aberarth, 1 mile north of Aberaeron.

Clamped to the wall of the west porch are two stone fragments. One has a pattern of squared fret with traces of an inscription and the other has some knotwork and diagonal key-patterns. They were found in 1860 during the rebuilding of the church and have been dated to around the tenth-century. Macalister in a surge of uncharacteristic enthusiasm called the original from which these bits survive as 'probably the finest cross in Wales'. In the church is a hogback stone of a century later, shaped like a recumbrant house with a curving roof ridge. Hogbacks are common in the north but apparently this sole find in Wales and of a type only found in Yorkshire remains unexplained in relation to Viking intrusion in the area.

Ref. ECMW No. 114; CCH No. 30, 31; CIIC No. 991; OS SN 476634.

Pembrokeshire

FREESTANDING CROSS, St Brynach's Churchyard, Nevern, 7 miles south-west of Cardigan.

Two different types of stone – Preseli dolerite for the shaft and the softer sandstone from which the wheelhead was carved – has produced a rather ungainly effect. The ornate wheelhead sits loosely by a mortise in a tenon joint on top of the 3m high quadrangular sculptured shaft. The top of the west face has been chamfered and the slight butt 1m above ground gives the effect of a 'base' on this freestanding high cross. Viewed from any side the green-hued panels have a variegated effect but in fact the carvings on the bottom are variations on the T-fret motif. The next four up are based on the knot as are the south and north faces of the next row while the east and west faces have fret patterns. The top four panels combine degrees of complexity of knotwork. The carving on the sand-stone crosshead is more intricate but still based on a limited number of motifs of linked oval rings, triquetra knots and the double-beaded two-cord twists that form the centre cross. An Anglian type, the curving arms are of expanded arcs beyond the moulded edges with four round pellets in the inter-spaces and a smaller boss in the centre of the main face.

Above the large knot of eternity on the western side is an inscription, DNS, an abbreviation of the Latin dominus Lord. Also found on a few Irish crosses. A panel with a jumble of half-uncial letters on the east face has an unknown meaning that Macalister suggested might be 'halliluia'.

Standing amid the gravestones beneath the low sweeping branches of almost equally ancient Irish yews the high cross is one of the few still to be seen in the traditional southern aspect outside the transept chapel. Its abstract sculpted panels and totally decorated cross-head show the mastery of Celtic religious art that was practised here by the late tenth-century.

Ref. ECMW No. 360; CADW-D No. 87; CIIC No. 1036; OS No. SN 083400.

CROSS-SLABS, St David's Cathedral, St David's

Part of a stone slab shows the left arm of a cross carved with elaborate double knotwork that ends in two birdheads with a small human head between them. Filling the top corner is a triple-winged seraph. The bearded? and tonsured figure sits within the triskele of the seraph's wings. Near to it on the wall of the south transept is a damaged stone with a decorated ribbon cross in relief and a Latin inscription dedicated to the sons of Bishop Abraham, who was killed in a Viking raid in 1080.

Other smaller fragments have Celtic patterns. Bits of stone mouldings and a curved pillar can be found at the rear of the nave. The decorated stones with fret and knot patterns may represent stylistic variations of the cross or parts of larger works, now lost. One stone, used as a gatepost in the past, shows a decorated outlined ring cross above an inscription of the name Grumarc in Irish lettering. Above it is: A7 W I(H)S XPS, 'Alpha & Omega Jesus Christ'. On the reverse side is a plain ring cross. These stones once graced a holy well on Pen Arthur's farm a few miles away.
Ref. ECMW No. 377, 376, 373, 374, 375; CADW-D No. 91; CIIC No. 1039, 1041; OS No. SM 751251.

Fragment of cross-slab, St David's Cathedral, St David's, Pembrokeshire.

FREESTANDING CROSS, Castle grounds, Carew, 4 miles east of Pembroke.

At 4.2m high and over 1.2m wide at its base, the buff-coloured cross is one of the tallest and least impressive in Wales. It is more of a visual and compositional mess than the Nevern cross with which it is often compared and dated to roughly the same period. They do share similar types of crosshead, decoration, a composite form and basic material as

Freestanding cross, Carew, Pembrokeshire. (Photograph by M.B.)

the shaft is from a long module of igneous Preseli dolerite, called a microtonalite. The crosshead too is of sandstone although the Carew has discoloured to a dullish brown and its thin slab which sits ungainly on the shaft has nothing of the robust quality of the Nevern crosshead. It has now flaked and the decoration almost gone. This upper section of the head and neck seems to have been modelled on some of the crosses at Margam and elsewhere in South Wales. In fact the main shaft itself with its large panels of plait and T-fret patterns to the break below the inscription is very similar in size, shape and decoration to the cross of Eiudon from Llanfynydd in Carmarthenshire which is now in the National Museum of Wales, Cardiff.

If Ralegh Radford's reading of the jumble of assorted letters is correct (and there have been quite a few different interpretations before him) as a memorial by Hywel to his brother Maredudd ap Edwin, joint ruler of Deheubarth the medieval kingdom of the south-west, then the composite aspect of work by different masons being brought together to create a grandiose monument would almost certainly produce the clumsiness and lack of proportion that characterises this cross. The irregular carving of a small range of Celtic patterns mixed with bland panels of over-decorative motifs emphasises Nash-Williams' observation, 'that it lacks at once the slender grace of the best of the Anglian and the massive shapeliness of the Irish high cross.'

Ref. ECMW No. 303; CADW-D No. 94; CIIC No. 1035; OS No. SN 047037.

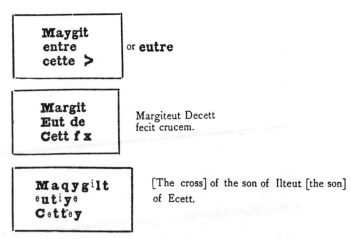

Interpretations by Westwood, John Rhys and others of the inscription on the Carew cross (from Little England beyond Wales by E. Laws).

FREESTANDING CROSS, St Nicholas Church, Penally, Tenby.

This elegant 1.9m high slab-cross is an unusual amalgamation of Northern decorative styles. The wheelhead and narrow shaft were carved from a single block of sandstone. The shaft spaying out towards the bottom has a slight butt at the unadorned base. The cross now in the south transept had formally stood in the churchyard. Its decorative crosshead, set within cable moulding, is composed of corded ring-twists formed around the central boss of a looped knot. The front and reverse are identical. The equally close similarity of design on both sides of the shaft is dramatically altered by a single vine-scroll of leaves and bunches of grapes. The vine-scroll is a conventional motif on Northumbrian crosses and its use here below the Anglian wheelhead suggests that the carver was attempting to synchronise these elements within a Celtic context, sometime during the early part of the 10th century.

Ref. ECMW No. 364; CADW-D No. 95. OS No. SS 117992.

Rubbing (quarter-size) of detail from Penally cross, Pembrokeshire.
(Photograph by M.H.)

CROSS-SHAFT, St Nicholas Church, Penally, Tenby.

Northern design elements are equally in evidence in this broken 1.7m high pillar of a freestanding cross from the same period. The vine-scrolls, confronting beasts, corded knotwork with a loose triskele that knots around a curved ribbon-animal are carved in a bold fashion within the heavy braided corners of the shaft that gradually narrow to the top.

The flaking of the surface that was so pronounced leaving much of the vertical bands of triple plait at the fractured top to stand away from the sandstone surface has been repaired. It is now placed at the back of the south transept, like the cross above, which only allows one face to be seen. In the vestry is a stone fragment with knotwork and moulded edges.

Ref. ECMW No. 363, 366; CADW-D No. 95; OS No. SS 117992.

Carmarthenshire

SLAB-CROSS, St Martin's Church, Laugharne, 4 miles south of St Clears.

The combination of bold design motifs inside a raised border of cable decoration has produced a surprisingly delicate stone cross. The equal-armed crosshead with four small triquetra knots in the interspaces is linked to a thick cable plait. Set out in high relief it forms a stem in the shape of an elongated knot of eternity. The inner design is encased in a raised decorative cable type border that follows the rounded shape of the flattish stone slab. This cross, less than two feet tall, is almost a miniature in contrast to most Welsh carved monuments. It has been dated to the early tenth-century and now stands in a niche inside the church.

Ref. ECMW No. 145; CADW-D No. 97; OS No. SN 301115.

CROSSHEADS, St Teilo's Church, Llandeilo.

Two ornately carved stone wheelheads nestle in the window of the north aisle. They are evidently all that remains of the high crosses that once marked out this important early monastic settlement or clas of St Teilo. The designs indicate a different type of head and perhaps even the form of shafts too, from those on the Pembrokeshire coast, bearing out the possibility of regional workshops associated with the main monasteries.

Crosshead in Llandeilo Church, Carmarthenshire.

Crosshead in Llandeilo Church, Carmarthenshire.

A squared equal-armed cross on both sides of one of the fragments is covered in a carved interlace pattern and set against a plain background with raised bosses on one face. The knot of plaitwork within each of the five square panels is placed within moulded borders. The interlace runs along the connecting arms and also within the arms. The other stone also has a squared cross on one side with traces of decoration. However the reverse face is rounded with an equal-armed cross ending in four rings with a smaller ring set inside. Within the terminals are four ringed bosses inside a circular border.
Ref. ECMW No. 155, 156. CADW-D No. 99. OS No. SN 629223.

Swansea

FRAGMENT OF CROSS SHAFT, St Cennydd's Church, Llangenith, Gower.

This elaborately carved sandstone slab now 1.4m in length and slightly tapering is set in an inverted position on the internal west wall. Located in the centre of the chancel floor prior to the restoration in 1884 it was referred to locally as 'Cenydd's stone' and probably used in conjunction with saint's skull reputed to be a relic here prior to the 16th century. The slab is filled with five rows of continuous knotwork that incorporates one central cruciform break. The design is carved in low relief and offset by edge mouldings. Two incised cross slabs are now on the walls of the vestry and on the lych-gate is a carving which depicts an incident in the *Life of St Cennydd*.

Ref. ECMW No. 209; RCAHMW No. 905; OS No. SN 428914.

Also on the Gower, in Llanmadog Church is a crudely shaped stone cross with an incised Latin type on the face; and in Llanrhidian Church, dedicated to St Illtud, is a fragment of a sculptured slab known as the Leper Stone. It is decorated with human and animal figures with a saltirewise cross on one face of what was a massive piece of limestone found embedded in front of the west tower doorway, late last century.

DECORATED FRAGMENT, Royal Institution Museum, Victoria Road, Swansea.

This coarse sandstone slab, broken and fragmented on all edges, shows a figure with both arms raised in the traditional *orans* praying position. The round 'Celtic' head and moonshaped face with eyes, nose and slit mouth simply rendered, adds to the impression of repose. A belted kilted skirt reaches to just above the knees and there are slight remains of what might be two bands of diagonal fret below the elbows. Above the 45cm long figure is a wide curved band of decorative carving that may have once formed the lowest squarend part of a cross portent. It was originally found not far from Capel Coelbren on Cefn Hirfynydd, near Neath, and is thought to have been the remains of a disc-headed slab-cross.

Kilted figures can be found on Scottish crosses. Recently another *orans* carving of similar dimensions has been found on a stone at Blaenawen in Pembrokeshire. Facial features of eyes, eyebrows and mouth are inscribed within a round 'Celtic' head and the body decoration is reminiscent of the Norse ribbon-decorated cross-slab at Nevern, four miles from the findspot.

Ref. ECMW No. 269; RCAHM No. 904; OS No. SS 679977.

Neath, Port Talbot

DECORATED SLAB, St Catherine's Church, Baglan, Port Talbot.

An ornate circular carving of double plait set in false relief of four loops to form a cross. At the top and bottom squared knotwork patterns break up the symmetry of the main design. At the bottom right is a Latin commemoration + BRANCU F. The slab which measures 70cm x 43cm was found last century in the churchyard of the ruined church of St Baglan. It is now set in the internal vestry wall of St Catherine's. In the *Life of Lleuddad*, the saint, particularly connected with Ynys Enlli *(Bardsey Island)*, was said to have been the son of Bryn Buga of Usk, who followed his (soul) brother Baglan into the religious life. The bell and crozier, traditionally associated with Baglan, is further indication that this site may have been an important religious centre.

Ref. ECMW No. 191; CIIC No. 1005; RACHMW No. 886; OS No. SN 753922.

CROSS SLAB, Parish Church, Llangyfelach, 4 miles north of Swansea.

The cross is an elaboration of a Latin type with arms and shaft formed from a continuous double ribbon carved in false relief. It is interlaced at the centre and the ends, beyond the knotwork ring, are squared in a double knot. The 110cm x 57cm wide cross has been cut down from a larger slab of gritstone. A distinctive Latin inscription runs alongside the stem in rounded half-uncials, CRUX XPI, The cross of Christ.

Dated to the ninth-century, the cross slab was originally found to be set in the floor of the church in 1913. It has since been re-set on the north wall of the nave. Another cross slab (1.32m long) forms the lintel of the door of the tower. An equal-armed cross set in a slightly recessed panel, it has four rings and hollows in the interspaces with a short stem, carved in slight relief.

Ref. ECMW No. 211 & 213; CIIC No. 1010; RCAHMW No. 882 & 883.

DECORATED PEDESTAL. Churchyard, Llangyfelach, 4 miles north of Swansea.

A socketed base of a high cross was raised up from the ground of its present position about seventy years ago, south of the tower of the old church. The narrow carved strip around the rectangular top of the 76cm high stone can now be clearly seen. A socket 48cm x 30cm x 33cm deep was cut into the sloping top of the stone, indicating the original cross may have been quite tall. It now has a modern stone covering.

The knotwork on the north side of the base is carved knot of eternity in low relief with pellets of different sizes in the interspaces. They help to balance the rather uneven plaiting and shows the 'hand' of the mason coping with a rather difficult gritstone block and probably carving it in

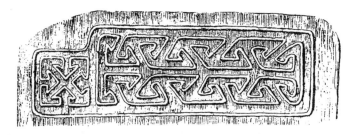

Pedestal in Llangyfelach churchyard, Swansea.

situ. The reverse side (114cm long) has a double band of triangular key-pattern that is repeated more regularly on the west face. On the east face is a knotwork pattern that forms four Stafford-knots with end loops. An early tenth-century date has been suggested. Unlike Ireland, such freestanding cross pedestals are not common here, and the others in this area of Wales are on the wheelcross at Margam and on the Cowchurch cross.

Ref. ECMW No. 212; RACHMW No. 931; OS No. SN 646989.

FREESTANDING CROSS, Margam Stones Museum, Margam, Port Talbot.

The Cross of Confelyn was carved from two separate blocks of local Pennant sandstone. Head and shaft were fitted to the base, much of which has now weathered. Romilly Allen noted, when casts were being made from it for the National Museum, that the shaft had sometime previously been shortened by a few inches and the pedestal recut for a new tendon and then reversed.

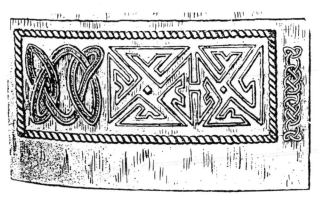

Pedestal of Cross of Confelyn, Margam, Port Talbot.

The wheelhead of the four-feet wide disc-headed cross is formed by a ring of interlace around an equal-armed cross of squared ends. Within the centre square is a raised boss that is surrounded by a separate chain of knotwork, noteworthy in that the loops are wider on the left. Perhaps from carving the stone upright (in situ?) or in making allowances for the offcentre effect of the boss. The plaitwork within the cross itself continues downward to form the stem that has figures on either side surrounded by motifs of triquetra knots and snakes. They are usually thought to represent St John with the Virgin Mary on the right hand side of the cross. However the one on the right seems to have a tonsured haircut with a snake around the neck while what appears to be a dragon sits on the head of the kingly figure on the left. Robes or perhaps a great cloak is held by a square clasp across the chest which could be a reliquary or shrinebox that were often carried around the neck of a bishop on special

Front of freestanding Cross of Confelyn, Margam, Port Talbot.

121

occasions. There are a number of inscriptions in rounded half-uncials on the front that contains the name CON/BELIN and an eroded one on the top of the outer ring of the cross.

The back of the cross is more weathered. What remains of its knotwork, interlacing and T-frets has a slightly freer more decorative feeling to the carving. On the base is a curious scene representing the chase? Set within a corded panel; a number of dogs seem to be bringing down a stag with a man on horseback carrying a shield, followed by a second horse with a knot (?) on the saddle. Right and left sides have panels of plaitwork and on the front of the base are three panels of T-fret and a double-knot.

Ref. ECMW No. 234; CIIC No. 1016; RCAHMW No. 907; CADW-G No. 73.

This cross of the period between the late ninth and early tenth century is considered to be the most accomplished of all the decorative high crosses in Wales. It was first noted as standing outside the churchyard against a cottage wall; then moved into the ruined abbey before finally being re-set in the museum in 1932. Since then it was the centrepiece of the lapidary collection in the small airless damp schoolhouse by Margam Abbey. The carvings span almost a millennium in time and styles from the re-used early Christian CANTUSUS dedication on a Roman pillarstone to the late radial wheelhead crosses and in many ways is a more impressive collection of representative crosses than those at the National Museum in Cardiff. But since they were packed so close together it was difficult to fully appreciate the finer points of design and decoration. The current re-building programme by Cadw should change this situation.

DISC-HEADED CROSS, Stones Museum, Margam, Port Talbot.

The Cross of Einion carved from a sandstone slab is 1.88m high with a circular head 71cm in width that has been trimmed-off at the edges. A border of triangular-fret forming a ring-cross sets off the equal-armed square-end cross decorated with six-cord knotwork. It links together at the centre around a small panel with two intertwining loops. A plain edge moulding sets off the wheelhead which sits compactly into the slightly splaying shaft. Below a large panel of triple strand plaitwork are two smaller panels of T-fret and a Latin inscription in five lines of half-uncials. It reads CRUX XPI (the cross of Christ) + ENNIAUN (made it for the soul of) GUORGORET. The reverse side is plain except for an incised

Shaft of Cross of Einion, Margam, Port Talbot.

Latin cross that covers the face and extends down the shaft. The decoration and form of this cross is similar to that of the Rhys Cross at Llanilltud Fawr and both are dated to the same period as the above.

Ref. ECMW No. 231; CIIC No. 1014; RCAHMW No. 908; OS No. SS 801864.

SLAB-CROSSES, Margam Museum, Margam, Port Talbot.

The Cross of Grutne has a deeply moulded but plain circular wheelhead of the Anglian type on a splayed shaft that is filled with a Latin inscription. The cross was carved from a single block of local sandstone and stands about a metre high. It has a tenon cut into the base but the socketed pedestal is missing. It once stood south of the church. The half-uncial lettering is crude and without spacing for the words which tells us that the cross was prepared (carved) by Grutne for the soul of Anest.

Another slab with its edges trimmed has an Anglian type crosshead with weathered knotwork that was linked around a centre boss. The deeply recessed plain interspaces and edge moulding around the ringed cross would have emphasised the importance of the cross rather than the panel below it, of incised lines around a nondescript irregular carving. The reverse face is weathered but with the remains of a cross formed by panels around a centre boss.

Ref. ECMW No. 233 & 235; CIIC No. 1015; RCAHMW No. 910 & 909.

RADIAL-CROSS SLABS, Margam Museum, Margam, Port Talbot.

There are two of these chunky rectangular slab crosses with sunken crossheads formed by eight spokes of a wheel radiating out from a raised boss. Due to their characteristic design or what we might call a 'logo' of Maltese form on both faces, are thought to have been boundary markers of the church. Both were, according to Edward Lhuyd, used as a footbridge on a nearby farm. A similar cross type, found nearer Kenfig on lands that belonged to the abbey, is now in the National Museum, Cardiff.

Cross of Grutne, Margam, Port Talbot.

Radial slab-cross of 'Illquici', Margam, Port Talbot.

The crosses of Illquici and Ilci, so named from what is considered to be proper names on their respective inscriptions, are sculpted although the former is more ornamental and less weathered than the latter. The area between the ring of the cross and the heavy mouldings has an irregular pattern of wavy lines that enclose two small spirals at the top. A faint inscription occupies the large panel beneath. The opposite face is similar with a slightly less ornate design around the wheelhead but with an incised equal-armed cross beneath it. The other sandstone slab is of the same thickness 25cm but slightly smaller at 1.65m. Weathering has reduced the original design considerably although the sides are merely incised with a waving line. Its worn inscription is in half-uncial lettering with dots separating the words however it is not certain if the Ilci 'who made the cross' lacks an initial letter.

Ref. ECMW No. 236 & 237; CIIC No. 1018 & 1019; RCAHMW No. 939 & 920.

STONE BASE, Margam Museum, Margam, Port Talbot.

The decorated panels of the quadrangular 1.2m high sandstone block are weathered. Apart from the back which is plain the three sides repeat a curious and not very interesting circular pattern that also covers the thick moulded edges. A large socket at the top of the shaft once held a missing stone cross-head which may have once stood near a holy well at Pen-yr-allt, on the Ogmore river a mile from Bridgend, from where the base was moved in 1969.

Ref. ECMW No. 252; RCAHMW No. 936; OS No. SS 801864.

Bridgend

PILLAR CROSS, St Roque's Chapel, Merthyr Mawr, Bridgend.

A weathered ringed cross-head on a squat rectangular shaft, carved from a single block of sandstone, stands inside the ruined chapel. It had been moved from at least two different places in the locality of Merthyr Mawr and as well as the broken head, part of the base has fallen off. It stands over 2m high and the original diameter of the crosshead was 96cm.

A looped double plait forms a triquetra knot on the remaining splayed arm – and which presumably decorated the two missing arms – to enclose a raised central boss on both sides. The thick edge moulding emphasis the hollowed arms and recessed plain ring. The end arms and

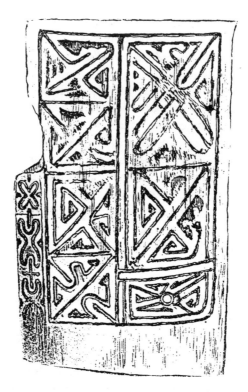

Shaft of pillar-cross, St Roque's Chapel, Merthyr Mawr, Bridgend.

outer part of the ring are thought to have been originally decorated. A vertical rib at the bottoms of the crosshead sets off the heavy roll-over mouldings on the top and sides of the shaft. On the 'front' a framed panel is filled with a Latin inscription which is now very weathered although it is thought that it may have recorded some kind of land transfer. The other side consists of a series of worn panels carved in diagonal key-patterns.

Ref. ECMW No. 240 CIIC No. 1022; RCAHMW No. 928; OS No. SS 880786.

INSCRIBED PILLAR, St Roque's Chapel, Merthyr Mawr, Bridgend.

A 1.22m high sandstone block is carved with plait and loose interlacing on three side with a long Latin inscription filling the remaining face. The missing letters of the first word CONBELANI are evident in a sketch made by Edward Lhuyd in 1697, a name which also occurs on the Great

Cross at Margam. The cross here was erected by him 'for his soul, for Saint Glywys and his brother and father'. The sketch also included a rough shaped crosshead that may have been similar in shape to the above but there is no further record of it. From the broken fragmented condition on the top of the pillarstone, it looks as if the crosshead was smashed off.
Ref. ECMW No. 239; CIIC No. 1023; RCAHMW No. 927; OS SS 880786.

CARVED SLAB CROSSES, St Teilo's Church, Merthyr Mawr, Bridgend.

In the lean-to shelter behind the church are a collection of carved stone crosses and fragments with incised outline Maltese crosses. This cross type is also found around St Dogmael's Abbey in Pembrokeshire but particularly common throughout Ireland. Peter Harbison (1991) has suggested that such crosses were part of the twelfth-century pilgrimage movement and were memorial stones in the sense that they were commissioned by pilgrims who had completed a pilgrimage. If this was the case at Merthyr Mawr then such an important religious shrine would have had its own sculpture workshop.

A 1.64m high rectangular block has a worn carving of a Maltese-type panelled cross radiating from a hub on one side surrounded by some patterning. It also had an inscription on the lower half. A smaller slab with a rounded top has a similar cross formy with a circled inset as the hub and surrounded by a ring of loose fret patterns. On the reverse is a worn cross of the same type.
Ref. ECMW No. 241 & 242; CIIC No. 1021; RCAHMW No. 917 & 918; CADW-G No. 75. OS No. SS 882774.

PILLAR CROSS, St Crallo's Church, Coychurch, Bridgend.

Falling masonry from the church tower in the late 19th century broke this 3m tall churchyard cross into three parts. Reassembled it is now inside the church. The double beaded loops with triquetra knots around the centre boss of the worn wheelhead appears similar to that at Merthyr Mawr. However the surrounding ring has been broken off and the wheelhead with an enlarged decorated plinth sits on a collar on top of the shaft. Its upper section has been completely worn of decoration or even by redressing as the lower part and the pedestal base were added in the fourteenth-century or thereabouts to modify it into a churchyard cross. The original upper sections have been dated to the late tenth or eleventh-century.

From the same period is a four-sided 1.62m high shaft, now also inside the church. The faces are recessed with deep angle-mouldings, one of which still has traces of carved plaitwork. The panels with some T-fret and looped knotwork are exceedingly worn as is the inscription on the east face.

Ref. ECMW 194 & 193; CIIC No. 1008 & 1009; RCAHMW No. 934 & 935. CADW-G No. 80; OS No. SS 940797.

Vale of Glamorgan

DISC-HEADED CROSS, St Canna's Church, Llangan, Cowbridge.

The graphic scene of the crucifixion of Christ is a rare Welsh example of its type. Figure portrayal on the cross-slabs around Brecon is usually schematised, more the 'stickman' variety than a truly symbolic representation. The front of this 1m wide cross-slab shows Christ transfixed, looking outward with a beard (?) and wearing a loin-cloth. The lance and sponge-bearer Longinus and Stephaton are below the outstretched arms in crouching positions within the weathered circular ring, against a sunken inner panel. At the top of the shaft beneath the ring is a smaller figure in low relief facing front with arms extended holding a small object in the right hand and the left hand has a curved horn or bow. This may represent Mary Magdalene, holding a horn or phial of ointment, as she is shown beneath the crucifixion on the tall Anglo-Saxon crosses at Gosforth and Ruthwell. The other side of the cross is equally weathered and has a sunken panel with an equal-armed cross in relief, surrounded by a plain ring.

Disc-headed cross, St Canna's Church, Llangan, Cowbridge, Vale of Glamorgan. (Drawing by M.H.)

The head and shaft – 1.3m high x 18cm thick and dated to the late ninth or early tenth-century – were carved from a block of local sandstone. The original socket stone is missing and the cross has recently been reset in concrete under a wooden shelter at the west end of the churchyard. Before it stood by the outer west wall of the church. Inside is an incomplete and broken slab in three pieces of sandstone – forming a ring cross(?) and part of a shaft(?). The 1m long slab has traces of a cross on the back.

Ref. ECMW No. 207 & 208; RCAHMW No. 913; CADW-GG No. 77; OS No. SS 957778.

DISC-HEADED CROSS, West Church, St Illtud's, Llanilltud Fawr.

The Houelt Cross is one of the most striking of the Celtic high crosses, as well as one of the earliest in Wales. Both sides of the large circular head and splayed shaft are carved with intricate fret decoration. Even the rim at the top of the head has remains of a band of key-patterns which probably covered all sides. In the Latin inscription on the front of the shaft, the Houelt who prepared it for the soul of his father Res is thought to have been Hywel ap Rhys whose death was recorded in 884. He was king of Glywysing, a territory between the river Tawe and the Usk.

The 1.9m high cross was carved from a slab of local gritstone but at present it is fractured front and back at the bottom of the 81cm diameter head and stands in the west nave of the church. The front of the head has an equal-armed cross of key-patterns with squared ends that sit within an outer ring of plain twists. Between the centre and outer squares of the cross are double beaded triquetra knots twisted to fit the interspaces. In keeping with the suggestion of a ringed cross portent in relief, the compact diagonal key-patterns on the shaft creates an almost kinetic illusion of movement. The front and rear carvings of the crosshead are identical, almost a mirror-image of each other. Two large panels divide the other side of the shaft with a triangular fret pattern above an ornate rendering of two Stafford knots joined by paired loops.

Ref. ECMW No. 220; CCIC No. 1011; RCAHMW No. 911; CADW-GG No. 74; OS No. SS 966687.

CROSS-SHAFTS, West Church, St Illtuds, Llanilltud Fawr.

Weathering has flaked much of the surface decoration from the face of the 3m high 'Samson Cross'. However the sides are covered by small panels of fret and loops that slightly taper towards the top and the reverse side of the shaft has a large panel of knotwork above a regular plait. In between these decorative panels are Latin inscriptions on the front and back in rounded half-uncials. The top of the shaft measures 58cm wide x 24cm thick and has a deep rectangular countersunk mortice which held the missing crosshead. It may have been a disc type similar to the above for there is a slight concavity at the top and the tapering regular panels could have been offset by a contrasting design on the crosshead. The front inscription in two panels records that Samson placed his cross/ for his soul; and on the reverse side, the founder saint, Samson the king, Samuel and Ebisar are commemorated. The shaft once lay outside by the path on the north side and when raised two skeletons were found beneath it.

Ref. ECMW No. 222; CIIC No. 1013; RCAHMW No. 912; CADW-GG No. 74.

CROSS-SHAFTS, West Church, St Illtud's, Llanilltud Fawr.

The south face of a four-sided block of local sandstone 2.75m tall is almost entirely covered by a Latin inscription of twenty-one lines. The cross was prepared by Samson the abbott for his soul and the soul of Iuthahelo the king who has been identified with a king of Gwent whose death was recorded in 848. There is a narrow vertical panel of carved plait on the right-hand side and at the base is a smaller carved square.

A 1.44m high shaft of sandstone has decorated panels on all four sides that taper towards the top. The bottom is slightly butted but both the base and the crosshead are lost. The decoration within recessed moulded panel is of double-knotted plaitwork of various complexity.

Ref. ECMW No. 223 & 221; CIIC No. 1012; RCAHMW No. 933 & 932.

Until the restoration at the beginning of this century the collection of stone crosses inside the West Church of St Illtud's were outside in the churchyard surrounded by tall palms. They joined the effigies, cross-slabs of long buried monks, stone coffins and sepulchral stone memorials to the dead. An old photograph in the church guide shows it like the horror house that was described just over a century ago, 'as a sepulchre, a charnal . . . the floor unpaved, in the midst are graves . . . an indescribable faint odour oppresses us. A gruesome place indeed.'

The West Church was built by the Normans on the original Celtic site. It was famed as a teaching clas and from the quality of the early medieval sculpture that spans a period from the ninth to the eleventh-century, it possibly included a school or mason's workshop. The East Church was erected in the thirteenth-century as the place of worship for the canons of the monastery. Restored and altered over the centuries, it was described by John Wesley in 1777 as the most beautiful and spacious church in Wales. With its arched wooden roof, wall paintings and elaborate stone altar screen, it is a verdict that can be echoed by the modern visitor.

PILLAR-CROSS, St Dochdwy's Churchyard, Llandough, Penarth.

A sketch by Edward Lluyd suggests that part of the crosshead was in place at the end of the seventeen-century. However his symmetrical shaft and central knop, but without its base, bears little likeness to the bulging exaggeration of the 3m high stone pillar in situ now. The surface of the extravagant angle columns is a twisting conglomeration of knots and plaitwork. The massive column is formed of five horizontal bands of stepped ornament and the base is surrounded on all sides by an overlarged cable moulding. The remaining part of the 58cm shaft has thick side moulding capping the four vertical decorated panels. Such a combination shows the baroque expressionism of high cross carving in South Wales by the close of the early medieval period.

Its four parts were carved separately from local Sutton stone that came from the old quarries at Ogmore-by-Sea. The rectangular pedestal is quite uneven with traces of decoration on the moulding. Each panel has figure carving on all four sides. The west panel has a man on horseback with a link of oval rings beneath the legs. The north side has a bust of a man between two sets of plait, a motif that is repeated on the south side. The east panel has five seated figures in a row holding staffs and a sceptre. The meaning of these figures, like the IRBICI inscribed on the front of the shaft is at best conjectural.

Ref. ECMW No. 206, CIIC No. 1007; RCAHMW No. 938; CADW-GG No. 78. OS No. ST 168733.

Cardiff

PILLAR CROSS, Llandaff Cathedral, Llandaff, Cardiff.

The 88cm tall shaft and head is all that remains of a composite high cross and gives some idea of what the finished Llandough cross might have looked like. The heavy edge moulding comes halfway up the shaft and then continues as a single roll moulding up and around the head. The decoration on the face is composed of an equal-armed cross with splayed ends around a raised damaged central boss. The linked knotwork in relief continues down the shaft. The reverse is much the same and on the sides is a plain knotwork strip which continues around the cross-arms between the moulded edges.

The cross stands in the south aisle on a block of stone which records how it was found in the wall of the Dairy Well (also known as St Teilo's Well) by the Bishop's Palace in 1870. Its original location is not known.
Ref. ECMW No. 205; RCAHMW No. 937; CADW-GG No. 76; OS No. ST 156779.

CROSSES & FRAGMENTS, National Museum of Wales, Cardiff.

The collection of the early Christian monuments on permanent display include casts of most of the major crosses described here and a small number of original stones (below) decorated in the Celtic manner. The complete list is included in *The Christian Celts, Treasures of Late Celtic Wales*, by Mark Redknap, published by the museum in 1991.

CROSS-SHAFT, Llanfynydd, Carmarthenshire.

Originally found in a field of stones called Aberglasney, the cross was removed to the town gardens of the Golden Grove estate in 1857. Later it was placed in the church at Llanfynydd from where it was taken to the museum in 1910. The location of the missing crosshead is unknown.

The carving on the 2m high freestanding shaft is an excellent example of the art of Celtic decoration. The motifs are all part of the common stock but it is the manner in which expanding panels of T-fret on the front are balanced against the double-beaded loops and centre inscription, EIUDON, that shows a master craftsman at work. The reverse has three large panels of loops, close plaitwork and a fret pattern that encloses a central swastika. One side has fifteen small panels of diagonal fret and

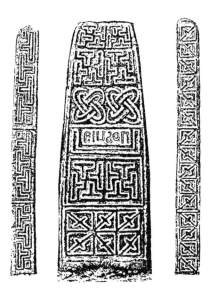

Front and side panels of Cross of Eiudon, National Museum of Wales, Cardiff.

the other is filled with Greek border fret. The use of highly contrasting panels, side fret patterns and an inscribed panel in front of half-uncial letters can also be seen on the 'Samson's Cross' at Llanilltud Fawr.
Ref. ECMW No. 159; CIIC No. 997; Nat. Gal. No. 30.

SLAB-CROSS, Pen-y-fai, Bridgend.

A weathered sandstone slab over 1m tall with a panelled cross formy carved in relief was found during ploughing in 1968. It was possibly a boundary cross, for the lands here once belonged to Margam Abbey, and its cartwheel of radial form can be seen on similar size and shaped crosses at Margam museum. Along the outer ring of the panel are two ringed pellets and the panel below has faint traces of an inscription. Below this is the undressed pointed foot of the stone 38cm long.
Ref. RCAHMW No. 922; Nat. Gal. No. 34.

SLAB-CROSS, Nash Manor, Glamorgan.

At the top of a narrow rectangular slab 2.65m tall is the representation of a ringed cross with shaft. In profile on either side two small figures with an arm extended to the cross give it an impression of overwhelming size. The square-end cross and ring are offset in relief by the hollow interspaces and a central roundel with a raised dot. There is some suggestion of decoration on the shaft. The rest of the slab has three ring-and-dots and a number of extremely weathered panels of biblical scenes. The reverse side is undecorated.

Ref. ECMW No. 250; RCAHMW No. 902; Nat .Gal. No. 26.

BROKEN CROSS-SLAB, St Dogmaels, Pembrokeshire.

The top part of the 1.52m high slab shows a deeply incised and large cross formy with a central ring. Complete it would have been nearly 1m wide. Beneath the cross is a faint figure of Christ, bearded, wearing a long-sleeved garment and with arms extended. This stone was found near St Dogmaels Abbey. Like other stone crosses there, it has been dated from the seventh to ninth-century. However the general use of such Maltese-type motifs suggests a later date especially if they functioned in part as boundary crosses on lands of the post-Norman abbey. Visited by Geraldus on his tour, it became an important centre on the Teifi estuary for the pre-Reformation St David's pilgrimage. (Pilgrim Ways, by J. Sharkey 1994).

Ref. ECMW No. 150; Nat. Gal. No. 14.

DECORATED SLAB, Caerleon churchyard, Monmouthshire.

A small portion of a broken slab shows carved knotwork on the right side, enclosed in the remains of two panels. On the left are two birds, one on top of the other, that may represent winged angels. Vertical panels of such winged birds can be seen on the broken fragments of a cross slab in St Arvans Church.

Ref. ECMW No. 291; Nat. Gal. No. 20.

Monmouthshire

CROSS-SLAB, Parish Church, St Arvans, 3 miles north of Chepstow.

Broken and weathered cross and shaft carved in slight relief on slab now in two parts. The upper part (50cm x 45cm) shows the sides and bottom half of an equal-armed square-end cross with looped ribbon decoration. A plain ring encloses the lower curved interspaces. The same decorative plaitwork continues down as the shaft and there are two panels of winged birds set on either side. The lower more weathered slab

(70cm x 45cm) shows the remainder of the shaft in relief and with two more bird panels on each side. The reverse side of the slabs has the same type of cross with a ring boss(?) but without any decoration. Alongside the shaft are knotwork vertical bands and with what looks like the remains of two rude scrolls or perhaps figures at the bottom. One of the 16cm wide sides shows some border fret.
Ref. ECMW No. 292; OS No. ST 540970.

Powys

PILLAR CROSS, Brecknock Museum, Brecon.

Before its present position in a tableau of inscribed and decorated Christian stone carvings from the locality, the cross had been moved to Maesmynys Church, about two miles from Neuadd Siarman farm where it had originally stood. Dated to the tenth-century, the 1.5m high cross is of a Saxon type found in southern Britain. The splayed arms of the wheelhead are delicately carved in knotwork around a sunken central ring. The moulded edging of the deeply scooped round pits sets it out in relief. The sides of the shaft have a tight vertical plaitwork decoration but the back is plain. The cross tapers into a slightly pointed and broken end. Another distinctive feature of the Neuadd Siarman cross is the regular bands of reel ornament along the rounded moulded sides.
Ref. ECMW No. 65.

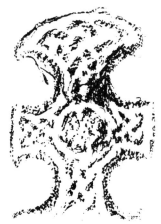

Rubbing (quarter-size) from wheelhead of pillar-cross, Brecknock Museum, Brecon.

BROKEN BASE, Brecknock Museum, Brecon.

A rectangular pedestal (65cm high x 32cm wide) from Erwhelm, Llanddewi'r Cwm. It has fragmented at the top where the carved pattern begins to form a regular plait from the more open knotwork that starts near the bottom of the base. All sides are similarly decorated. Nash-Williams suggests that the base may be the original of the above, also sometimes called the Llanynys Cross as both come from the same area, near Builth Wells. The latter place-name suggests an island llan or monastic enclosure on the nearby river Irfon.
Ref. ECMW No. 47.

Among the exhibits is a large wooden dugout canoe from Llangors Crannog. The artificial island in the lake, south of the modern village, was occupied during the Dark Ages. Fragments of bone, metal and leather work were found there but the most exciting find of the 1990 excavation was a rare fragment of closely woven cloth. The crannog is thought to have been the royal residence from where the wife of the king of Brycheiniog with thirty-three others were captured by the Mercians under their queen Aethelflaed in 916.

There are also a number of large impressive carved monuments behind the canoe. The Maiden's Stone with the eroded figures of a Roman soldier and his wife was discovered in 1698 during the building of a barn near Gaer Bannium. Then moved to the side of the Roman road where it was a landscape feature on the road into Brecon until it was installed in the museum. A massive red sandstone slab, nearly 2m tall, from Crickhowell has a clear well cut and legible Latin and Ogam inscription dedicated to TURPILLI. A cast of the large stone from Llywel church, near Trecastle, which is now in the British Museum has both Latin and Ogam inscriptions on one face. On the other side are a quartet of panels carved with lines, symbols and three 'stickmen'. One has what looks like a staff and another two crosses(?) on either side so they are thought to represent ecclesiastics. However the carving could be prehistoric and the stone which also has a large cupmark on the other side may have been a megalithic capstone prior to its reuse as sixth-century memorial.
Ref. ECMW No. 43 & 71.

CROSS SLAB, St Peter & St Illtud Church, Llanhamlach, 5 miles south-east of Brecon.

Two figures, male and female, stand with hands raised in the orans prayer position underneath the arms of a cross potent. The top part of the cross is missing but some border fret remains. The figures are surrounded by lines and beneath them are carved symbols of fret, a four-square and an open knot. Below these are large single-line loops that were repeated in double formation on the side. On the other side is an inscription stating that Moridic set up the stone. The carved portion is 1.16m high and the remaining two thirds of the slab is plain.
Ref. ECMW No. 61. CIIC No. 985; OS No. SO 089267.

CROSS-SHAFT, St Brynach's Church, Llanfrynach, 4 miles south-east of Brecon.

A long narrow shaft carving shows a figure with arms outstretched above a vertical band of interlace with a large cross set within the bottom loops. Below this are a set of triquetra knots. There is a short inscription on the other face.
Ref. ECMW No. 56; CIIC No. 981. OS No. SO 075254.

CROSS-SLAB, St Tyfaelog Church, Llandyfaelog fach, 3 miles north of Brecon.

One face of this 2.3m tall stone slab has an elaborately ornate design. Its four vertical sections are carved with a double-beaded Latin cross above a central warrior figure; a panel with a Latin dedication + BRIAMAIL and below it a rectangular panel of tight eight-corded plait. It formally stood in the churchyard, part of a vault, but it has been moved inside. The cross of double strands with flattened looped end-knots is similar in form to that at Llangyfelach church in Glamorgan but without its ring. There are four different kinds of knotwork above and below the arms, triple corded knots on the left side and double-corded on the right. The effect sets the cross in sharp relief. The full-frontal undecorated figure below it, is also offset by fret and knotwork filling all the spaces between him and the side moulded edges. Eyes, nose and mouth are clearly etched within the round head and he holds a sword with one hand and in the other is a mace or sceptre(?) over the squared shoulder.

The inscription appears to be unfinished although this may be the result of a different hand at work on a blank panel, as is the case with

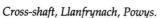

Cross-shaft, Llanfrynach, Powys.　　*Cross-slab, Llandyfaelog fach, Powys.*

other high crosses in Wales. The panel has a corded surround while the plaitwork below it runs right to the moulded edges. Dated to the late tenth-century it is certainly one of the more exciting examples of the carvers' art.

Ref. ECMW No. 49; CIIC No. 978; OS No. SN 034324.

PILLAR-CROSS, St Cynog Church, Defynnog, 7 miles east of Brecon.

The tall rectangular stone now stands in the porch of the church, formally it was in the masonry of the tower. It originally had an early dedication in Latin and Ogam and then centuries later was turned the other way up and a cross pattern carved on one face. Below a 20cm x 20cm carving of triangular fret set on the diagonals is a ringed cross of similar dimensions, also carved in low relief. Its present state may be due to weathering.
Ref. ECMW No. 44; CADW-CP No. 81; OS No. SN 925279.

PILLAR CROSS, St Meilog's Church, Llowes, 3 miles east of Hay-on-Wye.

Known as St Meilog's Cross, the stone was originally high on the Begwns, the hills to the north-west. It was moved and for nearly 800 years stood in the churchyard from where it was installed inside the church. A local legend claims that it was hurled down by a giantess and called Moll Walbee's stone before being carved into a cross. Meilog, one of the saintly sons of Caw, came from Strathclyde and founded a religious community within the present circular churchyard.

A ringed cross carved in high relief on the front of this 2m high stone is decorated with a series of raised diamond shapes along the arms and shaft. The largest of the seven square areas is at the centre of the wheelhead. A similar cross is on the reverse but plainer and without a ring. It has been dated to the eleventh-century.
Ref. ECMW No. 408; CADW-CP No. 80; OS No. SO 193417.

PILLAR-CROSS, Church, Bryngwyn, 5 miles north of Hay-on-Wye.

The top corner of the 1.7m high stone is missing. It has a deeply incised equal-armed Latin cross with rings and dots at the ends and at the centre around which the cross is formed. Four small crosslets are set in interspaces. The stone formally stood in the churchyard but is now inside the church on the south side of the chancel.
Ref. ECMW No. 405; CADW-CP No. 79; OS No. SO 186495.

PILLAR-STONE, Church, Carno, 10 miles east of Newton.

A curious incised ring-cross covers the upper face of the 1.5m tall stone. The equal-armed cross has a centre ring surrounded by a larger one from which are forked prongs touching the outer ring on the side of each arm.

The stone was discovered in 1960 as a gatepost over a mile away. Its original position is unknown. Like the previous cross, it has been dated on its form and style to earlier than the ninth-century.
Ref. CADW-CP No. 78. OS No. SN 963964.

SLAB-CROSS, St Tysilio and Mary Church, Meifod, 5 miles north-west of Welshpool.

The centrepiece of this carving is a large Latin cross set in relief and decorated with interlace that forms an elongated knot at the centre of the arms. Linked to the top arm is smaller wheeled Maltese cross with a figure of the crucified Christ inset on it. Four round pellets fill out the interspaces of the arms Decorative motifs of knotwork and a foliate border were carved alongside the crosses giving this tapering slab a diversified appearance rather than a coherent overall pattern. In terms of the linked crosses, iconography and formal decorative motifs there is a similarity to the carving on the east face of the 'marigold' cross in Carndonagh churchyard, Co. Donegal in the extreme north-west of Ireland.

Nash-Williams gave this cross a tenth-century date whereas Ralegh Radford thought that it may have been the coverstone of the tomb of Madoc ap Maredudd, a Powys prince who died in 1160. The church has always been associated with the ruling family whose capital was at nearby Mathafarn. The original site of St Tysilio was built between that of St Gwyddfarch and the present church. Prior to its position now at the west end of the south aisle, the slab was at the north end after it was removed from the top of a vault early last century.
Ref. ECMW No. 295; OS No. SJ 154132.

PILLAR-CROSS, St Dogfan Church, Llanrhaeadr-ym-Mochnant, 10 miles east of Oswestry.

A plain double-ringed Latin cross with slightly splaying shaft runs the length of this 1.7m tall rectangular slab. It is offset in relief by the surrounding carved ornament. A corded plait is on the left side of the shaft and on the right is a triangular fret pattern. Above the ring at the fractured top two spirals decorate the upper corners. A Latin inscription in rounded half-uncials is visible on the horizontal arm. The formula +XRI – the Cross of Christ – precedes a worn dedication.
Ref. ECMW No. 181; CIIC No. 1001; OS No. SJ 123260.

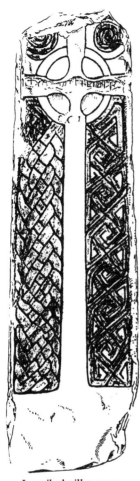

Inscribed pillar-cross,
Llanrhaeadr-ym-Mochnant, Powys.

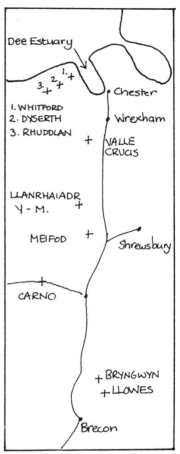

Dee Estuary

Chester

1. WHITFORD
2. DYSERTH
3. RHUDDLAN

Wrexham

VALLE
CRUCIS

LLANRHAIADR
Y - M.

MEIFOD

Shrewsbury

CARNO

BRYNGWYN
LLOWES

Brecon

Location of crosses in Powys,
Denbighshire, Flintshire.

Denbighshire

PILLAR-SHAFT, Llantysilio-yn-Iâl, Valle Crucis Abbey, Llangollen.

The decorative roll mouldings on top of the 2.4m high round pillar are all that remains of a high cross that was pulled down during the seventeenth-century. An inscription on the rear commemorates the re-erection of the pillar on a nearby mound in 1779, set in a square stone base. The extremely weathered text, copied down by Edward Lluyd in 1696, relates to the ruling house of Powys in the eight and ninth-century. It was king Concenn who erected the cross in memory of his great grandfather Eliseg, hence its more common name Eliseg's Pillar.
Ref. ECMW No. 182; CADW-CP No. 77; OS No. SJ 203445.

BROKEN-SLAB, Vicarage, Rhuddlan, 2 miles south of Rhyl.

The decorated stone rectangular block 70cm in length and 40cm wide has the remains of cable moulding on the front(?), indicating that it may have been part of a shaft of a freestanding cross. Above a pattern of a four-cord double-beaded plait is the bottom part a larger double-beaded knot. There is some weathered knotwork on the upper portion of the reverse side. A smaller stone block with similar carving may have been part of the same shaft.
Ref. ECMW No. 188. OS No.SJ 024779.

Flintshire

FREESTANDING CROSS, Churchyard, Dyserth, 5 miles south-east of Rhyl.

The remaining portion of the wheelhead shows it to have been a disc-headed type with a looped ring. The raised 13cm diameter boss on the east side is decorated with curved lines spiralling outward from its central point. Below it is part of a large double-beaded knot but the rest of the pattern has disappeared, apart from the triple-beaded knotwork that fills the bottom area of the shaft. The 1.7m cross is extremely weathered but the west side was decorated with an ornate three-corded looped pattern that is typical of Anglo-Viking carving, along these coastal regions to the north.

Freestanding cross, Dyserth, Flintshire.

The 50cm high five-sided pedestal is decorated with similar motifs and a ringed cross. It has a rectangular socket 30cm long and 18cm deep. It was found embedded in one of the walls during restoration of St Cwyfan's church and is now in the porch.

Ref. ECMW No. 185 & 186; OS No. SJ 112778.

FREESTANDING CROSS, Whitford, 4 miles south-east of Prestatyn.

Maen Achwyfan, the Stone of Lamentations, is carved from a single block and at 3.4m high is the tallest of the disc-headed type in Wales. Though not 'eared' like the above or the Penmon crosses, the wheelhead with its corded ring, triquetra knots forming a Maltese shape around an embellished boss is similar to those in Cheshire. The original influence was probably from the Isle of Man but the large Viking enclave in Britain during the ninth and tenth-century had its own established tradition of monumental carving.

Freestanding cross, Whitford, Flintshire.

The decoration on the shaft is similar to that of Northumbrian crosses. Its three large panels on the front are carved in low relief with a long vertical tightly corded ribbon plait, a squared key panel on a diagonal cross and at the bottom a series of spiral loops around an animal-headed figure. He holds an upright spear in on hand and in the other is a coiled serpent. The head and reverse side of the shaft is very weathered but the upper portion has a fine large double-beaded ring knot of eternity that is threaded through a four-corded loop forming a central ring. The sides of the cross have a more lively combination of carved decoration that includes fret, loops and knotwork, a dog with a spiral tail, a donkey with a curved tail that may have been part of the coiled serpent beneath and a figure in the centre of the south side with a rod(?) between its legs. The combination of Christian and heathen iconography is not uncommon on Northern high crosses.

The cross is in a field, fenced off for protection, about a mile or so west of Whitford village. It stands in what may its original position within a large flat stone base that has some scratch-marks on it.

Ref. ECMW No. 190; CADW-CP No. 74; OS No. SJ 129788.